Failing
Upward

Samarpan is a Hindu monk, teacher and writer of several books, articles and memoirs. He has delivered popular talks at various educational institutions and his orations on scriptures are available online both as videos and transcriptions. He teaches ancient and modern scriptures at the deemed university of the organization to which he belongs.

ALSO BY THE AUTHOR

SPIRITUAL FICTION

Tiya – A Parrot's Journey Home

Param

Junglezen Sheru

Kratu

PHILOSOPHY

Carving a Sky

RELIGION AND SPIRITUALITY

Living Hinduism

The World of Religions

The Hindu Way

Veda Vihangam – The Essential Veda

Arohan – Ascent with Gita

Failing Upward

SAMARPAN

PAN

First published 2026 by Pan
an imprint of Pan Macmillan Publishing India Private Limited
707 Kailash Building
26 K. G. Marg, New Delhi 110001
www.panmacmillan.co.in

Pan Macmillan, The Smithson, 6 Briset Street, Farringdon,
London EC1M 5NR
Associated companies throughout the world
www.panmacmillan.com

ISBN 978-93-6113-521-7

1 3 5 7 9 8 6 4 2

Typeset in Guardi LT Std by R. Ajith Kumar, New Delhi
Printed and bound in India by Thomson Press (India) Pvt Ltd.

FSC
www.fsc.org
MIX
Paper | Supporting responsible forestry
FSC® C010615

Srimat Swami Suhitananda ji Maharaj,
who always gave me an upward push
whenever I was failing down

CONTENTS

Preface

The desire to succeed is inherent in every being. It makes them train their young in the art of grazing their grass, which includes food, survival and mating.

In the case of human beings, this grazing may also take subtler shapes like art, music and other forms of creativity. The more sublime minds may even leave everything in the world for God.

For this very reason, the elders train us to succeed in whatever we are doing. In this process, they also teach us about the pitfalls that are spread liberally along the path. Sometimes we are mindful of these landmines and, at other times, we become too careless to protect ourselves. The result, in all these cases, may range from embarrassment to disaster.

As we grow, the supply of these cautionary notes decreases. Our obsession with success, unchecked by caution, leaves us vulnerable to both internal and external dangers.

Just like any other young person, I treated passion, action, drive and orientation as the primary factors of life. After years of stumbles, falls, injuries, moments of feeling crushed and shedding tears, I came to realize the folly of this outlook. I discovered that the Indian way of life, set apart from both common sense and nonsensical outlooks, approaches life with a different attitude and with greater precaution.

According to it, life makes a person spiritually strong enough to realize their true self. So problems, failures and falls are integral parts of one's existence; success and failures are merely exercises that build the spiritual muscles, enabling us to achieve anything, even God-realization. The world, thus, is a mere gymnasium where we build ourselves. It is neither for enjoyment nor for suffering.

However, not everyone can take failures in stride. Even worse, severe setbacks can cause mental health issues born out of a sense of hopelessness. At some point in life, some people develop a sense of meaninglessness and think of ending their lives. This fact is disturbing; nevertheless, it is true.

What to do to fix all this?

Away from the simplistic, quick-fix solutions to life's upheavals, the Indian way looks at life on a broader canvas that accepts failures and stumbles as part of growth and so cautions that whining, complaining, lamenting and shedding tears are actually a waste of time. The enduring message from India is: when you fail because of your own folly or due to the mischief of others, gather yourself, pick up the pieces of life and move upward. In life, there is no full stop, not even a comma; you are eternally what you are: divine.

This work, *Failing Upward*, is about the essential aspects of life that most of us pass through in our pursuit of success and happiness. It is presented as a free flow of ideas, more like a collage than an organized mosaic. Also, it is neither comprehensive nor preachy.

Those interested solely in life-building may go through *Carving a Sky*, but when they feel battered by life, this book may be of great help.

1

Failing and Failures

Whatever our outlook on life – Indian or Western, materialistic or spiritual – it takes us through the good and bad, which may drive us to plunge forward or shrink away. The common understanding of success is the ability to gather a large number of trophies in the activities that we consider good. However, we may fail repeatedly in the process. How do we handle setbacks when our sights are set afar? How do we go steady when the goalposts seem to recede as we proceed?

There are also occasions when all this appears inane and insipid; when life itself seems like a burden. What do we do then?

i

The world does not end here

I once happened to meet a devastated young lady, the mother of a baby girl. Her husband had died a year ago or so and soon after, she was forced into another marriage. The consequences were so devastating that she became suicidal. Her family members reached out to her, trying to calm her down.

When I tried talking to her, saying, 'Life does not end here. You will be born again and will start your life journey from where you left it.' She replied firmly, with tear-filled eyes, 'It all ends once the eyes are shut.'

Pretty painful!

She was well-educated and seemed to have great potential for the future. Yet she stood there, wishing to give up on her struggle. Only the love for her baby held her back. Somehow, we persuaded her to return home with her parents.

The incident left a deep mark on me, since life always gives a second chance. It also gives a third, a fourth and many more chances till we grow to our full potential. If it does not work out in one lifetime, life extends itself until the goal is attained. And yet, people firmly believe that 'it all ends once the eyes get closed.'

My favourite example is Dostoevsky, one of the greatest writers the world has ever seen. After reading his novels, *The Brothers Karamazov* and *Crime and Punishment,* I became curious about his life. As a young man, he was sentenced to death by the Tsarist government but his execution by firing squad was commuted at the last moment. The story goes that he vomited when he was released.

Imagine the loss to the world of literature had he died that day. Or even the loss to his own sense of fulfilment.

What was true for Dostoevsky is true for all of us. Those who think of self-execution should understand that life keeps giving new chances, if only you hold on to your capability. Even if you don't have a special talent like Dostoevsky, this life itself is a great chance to work toward a goal and raise yourself to be special.

India does not view life as a game of Russian roulette, in which one is either successful or a failure. It sees life as a continuum that flows through death and rebirth, starting from where we left off. In this process, it offers people experiences and an infinite number of chances, with the caveat that lost opportunities are lost time in pain and suffering.

The best thing for us is to get up, maximize our qualities and keep moving upward.

ii

Failing and falling may not be bad

We are only as great as our suffering.

Enjoyment is our comfort zone, so we assume that happiness is the aim of our lives. But no, it is not. The real goal is to outgrow our limitations and be great, which requires hammering and suffering.

Happiness is a state of rest, while suffering is a kick to get out of the rut. The sacred books of India are full of instances where sufferings, caused by failures, made a person great. Three stories illustrate this truth.

Dhruva is remembered as one of the greatest devotees of Lord Vishnu. The Pole Star is named after him because of his great devotion. The ancient stories say the universe revolves around the Pole Star which is his abode.

As a child, Dhruva once wished to sit in the lap of his father, the king, but he was scolded and stopped by his stepmother from doing so. With his pride hurt, he left the palace to seek the grace of God. The divine sage Narada tried to dissuade him but he failed, then he taught the boy how to pray and meditate.

Having learnt the art of higher life, he plunged completely and was finally blessed by the Lord. He became the greatest of devotees but also gained the kingdom and after his death, he attained the sacred abode.

Imagine Dhruva's life without him getting hurt for no fault of his!

On a different note, there is the story of Ahalya, who was the wife of the great sage Gautama. Her beauty drew the passions of Indra, the king of the gods. Ahalya too was tempted by his attention. When sage Gautama realized what had happened, he cursed both Indra and his wife: she would become disembodied and perform *tapasya* until Sri Rama, the incarnation of God, came and freed her.

After being in a state of suspended animation for years, she was released when Sri Rama visited her. She realized the nature of God, became a blessed soul and was reunited with sage Gautama.

If Ahalya had not committed this folly, she would have become a respected female sage. But because she fell and rose from the ashes, she is now adored.

Beyond 'not my fault' and 'sorry, it was my fault' is the story of sage Viswamitra. He was a king who quarrelled over a cow with sage Vasistha and got a major drubbing. Humiliated, he left his kingdom for *tapasya* just like Dhruva and Ahalya.

Due to the power of *tapasya,* he went on a spree of falls of different kinds, but he still persisted in his efforts. His final temptation was a divine *apsara* named Menaka, tempting him to his fall.

However, he never gave up. He persisted and became one of the greatest sages ever. One of his major contributions to humanity is the *Gayatri mantra,* along with his contribution of an entire section in the Veda.

His life shows how a person can grow to be great despite failures and obstacles. He was full of jealousy but became a great sage of peace, he was arrogant but acquired spiritual wisdom of inclusiveness and he fell into temptations but rose to become great in morality. The list goes on.

These three examples from the Indian tradition show that jolts and failures are often necessary to grow fully into one's potential. Every fall is, in fact, a portal to something greater, whether it becomes visible in this life. Or, maybe the next.

Indeed, pain and adversity push people upward. One only needs to persist in the struggle. Fail a hundred times, yet one success can make you great.

iii

Cry not, another life awaits you

As a young boy, I was a great admirer of Somerset Maugham's writings, whose works appeared to me to be above par. Charmed by his insights, I read all his stories and novels and some of them multiple times, which shaped my worldview. One of those stories is *The Verger*, about an illiterate verger (caretaker of a church) who had served a particular church for many years to everyone's satisfaction.

A time came when a new Vicar (stop-gap priest) was appointed, who was mortified to find that the verger was illiterate. Despite all his weeping and pleading, the verger was asked to leave, even though he was liked by all in the neighbourhood. Naturally, he was devastated.

Unfortunately for him, he knew no other work. With starvation staring him in the face, he opened a tobacco shop and over time, his business grew well enough for him to deposit his earnings in a bank. Once, when he needed to sign some papers, he gave the honest reply that he was illiterate. When the bank manager came to know of this, he said, 'And do you mean to say that you've built up this important business and amassed a fortune of thirty thousand pounds without being able to read or write? Good God, man, what would you be now if you had been able to?'

'I can tell you that, sir,' said Mr Foreman, a little smile on his still aristocratic features. 'I'd be verger of St Peter's, Neville Square.'

Indeed, we often don't know what lies within us until we get kicked out by the world. It is then that other forces open new doors for us. The intervening period between the two paths may be excruciating but there is absolutely no reason to give up.

If we have it in us, new doors will surely open. If we don't, then we need to 'carve a sky' for us.

iv

Act not foolishly during bad times to regret later

Balzac, the great French novelist and storyteller, has given us some fine pieces of literature. One of his novels that I loved hugely is *The Wild Ass's Skin (La Peau de chagrin)*, which depicts the plight of a young man who, in his despair, makes a bad choice only to regret it later, with no way out.

The story, set in Paris, is about a young man who is suicidal due to poverty. Recognizing his plight, an antique dealer gives him a magic piece, the skin from a wild ass, that would fulfill his every desire. But for each wish granted, the skin would shrink and consume a good portion of his physical energy, leading him to an early and painful death.

The story began with a sense of relief, humour and playfulness that soon turned into a mass of negativity, leading to imminent disaster that was impossible to ward off. Once the young man realized what was happening, he tried everything to get rid of that skin, which was rapidly losing its size, but he failed. The sheer terror and helplessness became too visible in his character every day and the folly of the escape route he had chosen turned into a deadly grave in no time.

It is not unusual for people to face desperate situations that turn their understanding into limp putty, leaving them open to bad judgements and disasters. That is how I have faced the suicide of a close friend and of a few other acquaintances. I have also seen people committing other kinds of follies that made them live with regrets for the rest of their lives.

Such incidents, bordering on stupidity born

out of despair or loneliness, hit many. In one of his books, the celebrated physicist Richard Feynman describes how, after the untimely passing of his beloved first wife, he sent a marriage proposal to a lady whom he knew well. They were not at all compatible, which he knew all along. But the decision, born of loneliness, as described by him, led him to an unhappy marriage that soon ended in a divorce, leaving a deep scar on his psyche. It was all lost time and emotions.

The way to avoid falling into such unnecessary traps is to have a close group of well-wishers in life. This requires investment in relationships, since these too need to be nurtured for a long time. Once there is a support system in place, trust it when making any important decisions.

However, the most important thing in staying away from the traps of despair is to remind oneself: 'Do nothing that you may have to regret tomorrow.'

Sometimes, we may think that we will not

live to see tomorrow but life has its own sense of humour; it makes us see another day and forces us to regret our haste for the rest of our lives.

V

It was not your fault: Shed a tear and move ahead

Many years ago, I was at one of our centres where we had a large dairy. To maintain the cows, it was our practice to purchase enough hay in the harvest season to last the whole year.

One evening, news came that the haystack had caught fire. The fire tenders came immediately but they could do nothing. I had a word with the firemen, who told me that in such instances they spray water to prevent other houses from catching fire and then wait for the entire haystack to burn down. There was nothing else they or anyone else could do.

The person in charge of the dairy kept

shedding tears. It was a big loss, as the hay had been purchased barely a month ago.

After a few days, we came to know that two kids of our staff, barely five years old, had found a matchbox from somewhere and were experimenting with lighting a matchstick. When they succeeded, they tried burning pieces of hay lying nearby. Soon, the fire started spreading, so they got scared and ran away. Out of fear, they did not inform anyone.

What could anyone do about this? Nothing.

This is true of life, too. At times, we face situations where no amount of precaution can save us from a nasty burn. The only thing to do after such a disaster is to shed a tear and move on.

This is true of the untimely deaths of our dear ones, too. What can anyone do about that? We may have to shed tears and blame our misfortune for a long time but ultimately, we have to move on. The important thing during such times is not to take any rash decisions.

vi

You may not even be in a problem

Many years ago, banking did not have modern gadgets, so all the work had to be done on paper. Withdrawals were a complicated process in which, when someone deposited a cheque, a token was handed over. That token, when presented to the cash counter, enabled the withdrawal.

The first time I went to a bank with a cheque, I was horrified to see the long queue, which was moving at snail's pace. Unfortunately for me, I had not paid attention at the token counter when the gentleman had asked me to go to a particular counter for withdrawal. Not understanding his words, I had instead stood in the long queue.

The wait seemed unending, during which I had noticed that a particular cash counter was free. I chanced to overhear the cashier telling a customer that he had only one token of a certain number. I checked mine and was embarrassed to see that it was the one. I rushed to that counter and got the cash in a minute. No queue, no waiting.

When I thought that I was in a problem, I actually was not!

A similar incident I read about long ago involved a boat travelling in the Atlantic Ocean, where the mighty Amazon river meets it. The boat needed fresh water, so it sent a desperate signal to a passing ship for help. The ship came near and when it heard the problem, the captain was surprised and said that they were in the fresh water already. The reason? River Amazon is so mighty that it pushes fresh water into the ocean for more than a hundred kilometres!

You can imagine the embarrassment of the adventurous crew seeking help.

Indeed, it often happens that when we think we are in a serious problem, there may be no problem at all. So, look back, check and consult to find whether you have a problem.

vii

Rejection is no cause for dejection

Failures and rejections have always been commonplace in life, giving rise to fables like 'sour grapes.' In recent times, as expectations from oneself and others have soared sky high, the rate of rejection and dejection too has skyrocketed, resulting in guilt, pain and a sense of worthlessness.

All this may be true for those who are flailing in the sty of materialism but those who know and follow the Indian way of life know better. For them, rejection is no cause for dejection, for it may stem from the worthlessness of those who are judging them.

There is a beautiful story that explains this idea.

Lakshmi is the goddess of wealth and prosperity in India. Her mount is an owl, probably because the truly learned never run after wealth!

Once, the goddess gave a divine necklace to the owl with the instruction that he should gift it to the most beautiful female in the universe. The owl flew to various spheres of existence, looking for the most beautiful being but he could find no one. He rejected all the goddesses, divine beings like *apsaras, yakshas* and others. From there, he came to the earth but there was no one worthy of the necklace.

Flying all around, he finally found a female owl in the cavity of an old tree, blinking her eyes. The owl was happy; he had finally found the perfect beauty!

When you get rejected by someone, do not feel dejected. Know that the other one may be looking for a perfect face in an owl!

Indeed, this is true. That is why we hear of great persons like Dr A. P. J. Abdul Kalam being rejected by many and even of great authors receiving countless rejection slips before becoming bestselling authors. Even the great Einstein, like many other scientists, faced opposition to his theories. The rejecting parties were in search of their perfect owls!

I have been fortunate to see and know quite a few people who became great after being rejected here and there. So, despair not and keep struggling.

2

Life Gives Signals

i

Stop and turn right

Ganga, the most sacred river of India, is where every Hindu wishes to wash away their sins in life and wants their ashes immersed after cremation for a better afterlife.

The story goes that King Bhagirath performed intense *tapasya* to bring Ganga down from the heavens to purify the remains of his ancestors, who had been reduced to ashes by a sage's curse. Long story short, when Bhagirath succeeded, he took Ganga through the ravines and valleys, over the huge boulders and plains. Thus, as she flows, Ganga appears at times furious, at times frolicsome, at times calm, depending on the land she passes through.

Rishikesh is one of the places where one can see the Ganga in her many moods. Near Rajaji National Park, the river flows tamely enough for a road to go through its bed. The driver must ensure that the water is not too high. I have taken that road a few times and loved it.

Once, while travelling that road with some friends, we were engrossed in animated conversation. Plus, it was getting dark. These two factors, darkness and engrossment, made us miss the road signal warning drivers to turn right and cross a bridge. A furious flood had washed away the old road some years ago.

As we continued, the road got more and more bumpy. Thinking that it was only natural as we had to cross the river bed, we continued slowly. There were now big crevices, holes and stray stones on the road. Worried, I got out of the car to check what the matter was. I looked around, only to realize that the occasional vehicles were taking a right turn, which we had missed.

Our capable driver slowly brought the vehicle back on the road. We then noticed the boards that cautioned about the broken road ahead. We heaved a sigh of relief that the water was not released from the dam at that hour! Or else a watery grave would have welcomed us.

What is true of this story applies to life, too. Whenever danger lurks, life often gives us warning signals. They only become louder as we proceed on the closed roads. It is we who ignore these signals and persist out of stubbornness, dragging us and our dear ones, into the dark and dangerous abyss of death or ignominy.

When a job, a relationship, a journey, anything really, grows bumpier, it may be time to turn back and take the right turn. When hurt and tears start to grow darker, it is time to get out. Ignore the signs and signals at your own peril. That alone is the way forward.

Interestingly, life also signals when we are on the right path. On many occasions, I received unexpected help and suggestions when a task seemed too difficult. There are more such stories than I can narrate here.

ii

Protect your back

Growing up in an Indian village in the twentieth century had its charms, despite its hardships and the lessons learned that were phenomenal.

Most houses then were made of mud. Burglary was common but often done in a different way. The burglars, known as *sendhmaar*, would dig a small hole and squeeze into the targeted house. Such holes were known as *sendh*, a word that is now used to indicate an unexpected side attack.

As a kid, I found it amusing that the thief entered feet first but came out head first. If someone noticed the intrusion or the exit, the burglar's legs would be caught or attacked, but he could still save himself. It is similar to testing the waters.

Life gives signals. So, even when a person moves into a danger zone, they must have their back covered, the way the burglars used to do. In army language, it is known as cover fire.

Those who get into misadventures without precautions often land in serious trouble.

3

Mistakes, Mistakes

i

Watch for the build-up

In most cases, we bring trouble on ourselves. The wrong that happens to us is mostly because we invited it upon us and worse, it does not happen in a day; rather, the build-up takes time – it may even go back to previous births.

Einstein's famous theory of relativity says that energy and matter have a fundamental interconnectedness and time and space are not separate but a continuum. What we often miss is that the build-up had begun centuries ago with Copernicus, Galileo and Newton contributing to the changing model of the universe from geocentric to heliocentric; J. P. Joule and James Clerk Maxwell showed the inherent oneness between the various, seemingly disparate forces of nature.

This is true in literature, sports, art, architecture and every other area of human excellence. What we call a grand work or a groundbreaking work may never be attained by one person and is contributed to by many who may often remain unknown. The slow build-up is often missed by ordinary minds, so it is notorious to conclude 'an event changed everything' or 'one person brought the revolution'.

To neutralize the blunders, one needs to look out for the build-up that signals us through portents, which is known as *nimitta* in Sanskrit. The word means 'sign/signal' and also 'the agent through which an act is accomplished'. So, when a cyclone hits an area, it is first preceded by a soft breeze, signalling the impending doom. The breeze is not the harbinger of the cyclone but the scream of warning for people to take shelter.

Absorbed in our self-interest, we often ignore such portents as coincidences. But if we pile up our mischief, it is a good idea to stay alert to the signals before disaster strikes.

ii

Saying sorry makes us great

Years ago, I heard from a senior monk who once met a government official during the British rule.

After the work was done, he took the official paper and left. Later, he was called back by the officer and scolded, 'It doesn't cost you anything to say, 'Thank you'.' The monk, terribly embarrassed, apologized profusely.

Later, I read an essay 'On saying please,' which begins with an incident where a lift operator throws a person out because he had not added 'please' along with his floor number.

In recent times, it has been popularized by the semi-educated that 'No sorry, no thank you'. This is plain bad. When you say thank you, you are expressing your gratitude to someone, even if that person is your great friend. It is a sign of inclusiveness and universal acceptance.

More serious than this is the idea of saying sorry.

In the journey of life, mistakes are inevitable and one must repent and correct them. Every religion makes its followers repent and/or perform penance. So, people confess and make pilgrimages to atone for their mistakes, whether they were committed unknowingly or deliberately.

There is no match for 'sorry' to those whom we wronged. Only those of strong character can say sorry and saying sorry makes one strong. For that, we have to muster up our inner strength and own our blunders. As kids, we lacked the strength but as we grow, we must have enough strength to admit.

Admitting our faults may cause temporary setbacks but, in the long run, can make us achieve big in life. Mistake or even sin is like falling into a moral sty. One has to first promise never to fall into that again and ask for forgiveness.

Asking mentally for forgiveness is a trick to fool others and ourselves. No one improves through that.

iii

Monkey's dead baby

Indian spiritual traditions repeatedly caution us not to be overwhelmed by sorrow as it's unavoidable. The idea is that our pain and sorrow may be caused by reasons one has no control over. But the consequences, such as brooding or moping over it, add to our misery.

Once, I was at a place with many monkeys. There, I learned that the alpha male kills his own male baby, his son, when born to a female. The grieving mom carries the baby's carcass, holding it close to her chest, until it rots and stinks.

When it comes to our own problems, we often end up holding on to our pains like the carcass of a dead baby by the mother monkey.

Some years ago, I once knew a gentleman who had a deep grudge against a colleague. He had collected a large volume of documents for all his wrongdoings. He planned to use those papers someday but it was deemed difficult because of his position. So when he narrated the stories with documented proof, I told him sternly, 'Look, if you have the guts, then go to the higher authorities and lodge a protest. Or else, throw all this in the gutter. Do not burden your head and your peace with all this.'

As expected, he stopped talking to me. A few days later, he came to me and thanked me for the advice. He sheepishly admitted that once he threw away the file, he was able to sleep well at night.

Moving around with unnecessary baggage, in the form of dead incidents and memories, becomes more acute as we get older. With nothing much to do, the elderly often dwell on the past and grieve over lost opportunities and missed chances. Even when we urge them to take up religious or spiritual activities to divert their minds, they seldom do so.

The true mantra, as Lord Jesus said, is to 'let the dead bury their dead.'

iv

You were never wrong but set it right now

There was a time when I believed that people make mistakes knowingly. Later, I felt that they do so unknowingly. Now, I know better. I am convinced that no one ever makes mistakes. They are simply convinced, at that point in time, that they are right, including mischief. It is only in the hindsight or when corrected by others that we realize our mistake, if at all we realize it.

As a schoolboy in my village, we were tempted by the ice candy sold by hawkers for five paisa each. But the elders forbade us from purchasing them except during fairs and special occasions.

One day, some boys from my school got it into their heads that the candies contained saccharine. We had no idea what that was but assumed it must be harmful. The boys started teasing him and one even ran away with his turban. I enjoyed the scene, not indulging in it, as I never had the courage for such things. A little later, one of my elder cousins came to know of it. He got very angry and severely reprimanded me for even being present there.

Surprisingly, what had seemed perfectly normal to me an hour ago now seemed like a criminal act. I regret it, even today.

Whatever we do, right or wrong, is always

done with the full understanding of rightness at that point in time. But as time passes, we may realize we were wrong. That is when we may set things right by apologizing, changing our way of life, or even going on a pilgrimage as penance. Whatever appears to be right.

There is nothing wrong in changing our opinion about an idea or a person when we finally realize our misjudgement. Admitting mistakes and course-correcting help us grow.

V

Missing tile syndrome: Accept the canvas

The missing tile syndrome is a popular concept in human behaviour where we tend to note the missing part of a pattern. When a tile is missing from the wall, we notice that. When there is a big black dot on a white board, we focus on the black dot.

While this attitude is normal, it is much better to have the complete canvas approach, where we create a collage out of the missing links.

Instead of lamenting missed opportunities and shedding tears on our failings, we can see life as a complete canvas and create new achievements for ourselves that would make life look like a new collage rather than a board with a missing tile.

In a poignant incident, a young man loved a beautiful lady. Unfortunately, the young man met with a nasty accident that left him crippled and helpless. The woman left him for a better person. The crippled gentleman then went on to create an out-of-this-world beautiful garden in memory of his lost love, despite his disabilities. With time, the garden came to be known as 'The Dead Man's Garden' and drew thousands of visitors every day.

One swallow doesn't make a spring, nor does one disaster create Hell.

4

Illusions and Delusions

The big illusion we all experience every day is the state of dreams. When we move from the world of objects to the state when the mind stops functioning, we are said to be in deep sleep. Irrespective of what scientists say, this everyday experience is universal and undeniable.

In the dream state, we create a new world of objects, people and emotions based on the accumulated impressions and imaginations of our life. Freud found libido and mortido even in dreams, but it is not so; dreams may also project our emotions and aspirations, including spiritual longing.

More interestingly, we often weave wonderful stories as we dream. Once I had read about a tribe where the family members shared a 'dream breakfast' every morning, recounting their dreams from the night. People capable of having lucid dreams know well the wonderful stories in that state. Whenever the story seems to get irrational or not to our liking, we tend to give the dream a different direction.

Surprisingly, what is true of dreams is also true of life. We can change its course when things tend to go beyond the set pattern that we want to have. Going beyond the set pattern is what we call illusions and disappointments.

For example, in the case of a collage, something extra does not make a difference, but in the case of a beautiful painting, even the faintest extra dot can be intolerable. Those who treat life as it comes, for them, there is nothing called illusion or aberration. But those who want life to be picture perfect, for them, anything out of the pattern is unacceptable.

Despite our efforts, we suffer setbacks, find a broken chain in the story of life and find missing pieces that give us the feeling of illusions and delusions. How to get rid of these is the subject of this section.

i

Two delusions: The world needs me, I need the world

Over the years, I have realized that we all have two major delusions:

1. The world needs me
2. I need the world

This idea may seem preposterous; nevertheless, it is true. Moreover, a lot of our pain and failure stems from these two illusions.

I knew a gentleman who, after retiring from a great job, chose to volunteer at a library where he dusted and arranged books.

Having worked there for months, he once needed to go on a trip and asked for leave from the librarian, who said, 'Of course, you can go. We do not need you here.' The gentleman felt shattered and devastated.

When he narrated the incident to me, I could not stop laughing, partly because of my youthful immaturity and partly because of the absurdity. I commented, 'How could you even imagine that you were important there?'

This is a problem with many of our lives; we push ourselves into something, only to realize late in life that no one needed us.

In a more heart-wrenching story, the great Sanskrit author Dandin narrates the story of Marichi and Kamamanjari in his immortal work, *Dasha Kumar Charita.*

Marichi, a great hermit, had grown old performing great austerities, making him famous. He also gained the power to foretell destiny. Once, a young, famous courtesan renounced the world and came to his ashram. Over the days, the sage was charmed by her dedication. One thing led to another and the damsel trapped him into swearing that he would marry her. Together, the old hermit and the young courtesan, reached the king. What a couple!

In the royal court, the sage learned that the lady had a bet with her friend that she could persuade the old hermit to marry her.

'What about our marriage, dear?' asked the sage.

'Go back to your ashram and your way of life,' replied the lady.

The sage, as if struck by the thunderbolt, said to her, 'Dear, what does this mean? Why this indifference? Where is that affection you showed me?'

She smiled and told how it was all about the bet with her friend and added, 'I won the wager because of you. Look at your age. Now, go back.'

The silly ascetic, feeling empty, returned to his dwelling with his lost honour, time, self-respect and his power to foretell the destiny.

Everything. All because he had wrongly concluded that the lady needed him, or worse, he needed her!

The story deeply impressed me. When a dejected person comes to me in pain, I always mention this story and conclude: we live in a delusion that the world needs us or that we need the world. But no one needs anyone. At best, our relationships are like crutches that help us walk through the slippery patches of life. Nothing more.

As mentioned earlier, there is never a full stop with the Indian way of life, so Marichi brooded over his loss for a long time but ultimately returned to his austerities and established his sagely glories again.

ii

We only love our own extensions

It has become a truism for the youth to declare that their love is 'unique' and 'they are going to be together for eternity.' Lucky is an impetuous young person if their 'uniqueness' can last even a few months.

In one of the Upanishads, Yajnavalkya, one of the greatest sages of India, explains to his wife, Maitreyi, that people love only themselves, *na vā are patyuḥ kāmāya patiḥ priyo bhavati, ātmanas tu kāmāya patiḥ priyo bhavat ...'* (Know that a wife loves her husband not for his sake but for the sake of the Self.)

The sage then lists many more things and explains how one's love for anything in this world is actually the love for one's own Self (i.e., the spiritual essence).

At the spiritual level, we love others because we see our own Self in it. At the lower level, it is our own Self that envelops the other and then we love that.

This is best understood with a popular story about coal theft from a railway yard. It was reported that a lot of coal was being stolen from a particular rail yard. When the British officer enquired, the local officers, who were hand in glove with the theft, claimed that the stray cows were eating the coal. To prove their point, the locals poured molasses over a pile of coal. The cows happily licked the molasses away. The British officer saw this from a distance and was left in disbelief at cows eating coal!

We are all like that. We pour our own love on some object or people and then lick it, convinced that it is lovely. When a person loves someone, they actually taste their own love but mistakenly attribute it to the other person.

There is no such thing as objective love in this world. What we love is only subjective love. Once we realize this, the chasing of the chimera stops. The wealthy man pursues wealth for the sake of his own Self, the king expands his empire for himself, the lover pursues the beloved for himself. The more passionate the pursuit, the more intense the self-seeking.

There is nothing wrong with chasing people, objects and dreams. But to rise higher, one must know that all this chasing is a mere illusion. It is then that one truly starts to live life.

iii

You are not responsible for the mess, so stick to your dharma

Immature minds identify themselves with anyone who comes near them, despite the initial hesitation. This may be fine in case of kids, but it is dangerous for adults who identify with all and sundry. The tendency to identify may be due to an overflow of love within, but it has the potential to damage the present hugely. Unlike the popular belief, people, particularly the emotional type, should always ignore what their heart says and instead follow what the mind says.

Dharma is the duty of a person based on their way of life. At the top of the priority list is spiritual growth, followed by the welfare of family, community, society, country, world.

Failure in life often comes when the chain of priority is broken.

In the sacred book, *Bhagavatam*, there is a phenomenal story of King Bharat, who in his old age, gave up his kingdom for a spiritual life on the riverbank. Once, he rescued a newborn fawn abandoned by its mother. The king-sage saved it, nursed it and in no time, got so attached to it that all his activities centred around the fawn. The attachment was so severe that he was born as a deer in his next birth! Of course, he finally became great in his next birth, but the pain during the interim period was really bad.

What the king had done was perfectly all right, but his untrained mind, overflowing with emotions, made him lose his priorities. This is where one's *dharma* comes to rescue and saves them from getting carried away by the unnecessary.

A senior monk told me, 'Whenever someone comes to you in crisis, talk, help and move away. Make sure to have no second interaction with those in the mess. That is not your way of life, not your *dharma*. You are not responsible for the mess that is in the world, so it is not your responsibility to set it right.'

Compassion leads to passions, if not regulated by one's *dharma*.

iv

Truant mind: The dog on the walk

Acting stupidly is the privilege of the emotionally immature. It mostly happens because:

1. People do not stick to their way of life.
2. They let their mind race ahead of the present.

For example, a gentleman who goes on a daily walk with his dog often follows the dog, who knows the route well.

Now, if the master, for some reason, changes his route, the dog will be disappointed but come back willy-nilly. Interestingly, it will do the same thing, again and again. After all, dogs are meant for running and not for peaceful walking.

Something similar happens to the mind, particularly to those who let the mind wander. Such minds keep racing ahead, concluding things and hoping for what they consider likeable. Unfortunately, the world has its own dynamics and so, the mind has to retrace its steps, which can be quite painful for the emotionally fragile.

Even those who step outside the boundaries set by *dharma* have the same problem. One funny thing about crossing the boundary is that one crosses it only because 'the grass appears greener on the other side.' Once it has been done, the grass not only seems greener but also fragrant, since there is nothing to hold one back.

The consequences need no elaboration.

V

We love our delusions

Albert Camus, a French writer and Nobel Prize winner, is another favourite of mine. In one of his classic works, *The Plague*, he describes a hypothetical civilization that lives in cold and hunger within a huge cave. When a person escapes, finds the warmth of the Sun and plenty of food, he rushes back to share his discovery but people ridicule him for such absurd ideas. There are the rare few who believe him but refuse to join him, saying that there has been a bread distribution announcement from the shop!

Deluded since our birth to believe that our 'frog in the well' existence is the real existence, we refuse to stir out of it. 'Nice words!' 'Quite soothing!' 'Unique!' are words used for those who strive for a better life, but when it comes to changing ourselves, no one cares about the way forward.

There was a time when I delivered a talk at a premier institute on 'Indian Ethos in Business Management'. Such talks demand time and energy, yet I went hoping that students might benefit from it. One day, I overheard two students talking after my session was over, 'Nice monk! We got to hear some words of *gyan!*' That was the end of my enthusiasm.

No wonder, Indians describe the world as *Maya,* meaning people will continue to love their illusions and delusions, shed tears in the hope of an occasional smile, starve in the hope of getting crumbs, die many deaths in the hope of getting a better birth, suffer in the hope of being heard some day ... This is what the world is and it will continue to be. People love to live in their sty.

Lucky are they who say, 'Enough! No more. I need to move upward.'

5

Be a Lone Warrior

Most of our pain, suffering, illusions and disappointments are simply because we are not aware of who we truly are and what we can achieve.

Throughout the world, kids are trained in schools and colleges to become useful cogs in the machine-like society and are told to believe in grandiose words like freedom and equality, without realizing that these two aspects of life can never co-exist. Equality means to have bonsai-like existence, while freedom is a tree in a forest, free to grow in height and girth. Expressions like 'We believe in freedom and equality' are tools of exploiting the naive by crooks.

Indeed, freedom can never co-exist with equality, since it requires only environment and not typecast drilling. This is true of art, science, religion: everything. No two individuals are ever, I repeat, ever equal. Due to this, drills, discipline and training are required to chip away the irregularity and speciality of personalities, making them a cohesive team, as in military. But even there, the individual quality does get expressed.

This section focuses on one's individuality.

However, individuality does not mean oddity but universality. Imagine a piece of wood in a wood factory. A plank there is as good as any other one there. Now, if a chair is made out of it, it has more universality, as a chair and also as wood. Thus, it has better individuality. If that chair is converted into an ornamented one, then into a royal chair, its universality and consequently, individuality would keep increasing. Individuality is used here in this sense only.

i

You are unique

The first step to growth is accepting that we, as human beings, are unique. Once we realize this then it will become a reality for us. But the problem is that we identify ourselves with the herd and yet think that we are unique!

This problem of identifying with the herd and its consequences intrigued me for a long time. *Junglezen Sheru* describes the plight of a lion cub that wants to be one of the herd, leading to devastating consequences. In contrast, the character of Homa in *Kratu* shows how Homa used to feel one with the herd but upon realizing the power of his wings, he never looked back.

The Fountainhead by Ayn Rand, one of my loved books, describes the personality of Howard Roark, a gifted architect. Although I do not accept Rand's philosophical outlook based on Objectivism, her portrayal of Roark is magnificent. He learns the nuances of architecture in college and then leaves without a degree to begin a career by himself.

Yes, we all are unique, for uniqueness is inherent in human beings. Let that not be a mere idea in the head but let it manifest in every act.

One of my favourite lines of inspiration has been *'ekla chalo re'* (walk alone) by the great poet, Rabindranath Tagore. Indeed, one has to be a lone warrior to go upward in life, just as every molecule of water has to separate itself from the body of water to move upward.

When we were young, we wished to be one with the herd but we must spread our wings. A look at the people from different walks of life highlights how no two people are similar. No two prophets, authors, scientists, philosophers, conquerors, artists etc. were ever similar. There may be some common factors but their uniqueness is unmissable. Their training and drills are limited to teaching them how to avoid the pitfalls along their path, much like how Ramanujan was trained by Mr Hardy in mathematics, yet their achievements are unique.

Even when your ideas are borrowed, the way the greats express is always unique. The basic ideas in some of the Kalidasa's works are sourced but his creations are unique.

No one may come to help you and many more may never understand what you are doing. Just build your inner strength and let your personality bloom with your true nature.

Uniqueness lies in originality but is based in universality. As you move ahead, people will join you.

ii

Have a myth, have faith

Once a friend commented, 'God is a myth!'

I said, 'Indeed, the world too is a myth since the instrument of knowledge in both cases is the mind.'

One of the greatest mysteries in life is how we consider dreams and imagination to be false, the waking state to be true but the instrument of knowledge, in all states, is the same mind. Away from our world view, many philosophers and sages have taught that the world is not as real as it appears to be. Take a whiff of any opioid and you will see how the perception of the reality changes!

Whatever the reality, life does not run like a railway train with wheels trapped within the two rail tracks. It can change its course whenever, implying that there is no fixed reality and hence, there can be no fixed rules in life. One can and should do whatever suits their growth. As mentioned earlier, no two paths will ever be same.

A great way to grow is by having a personal myth. It's not about having an ideal but being rooted in personal belief about oneself.

Myth is a much-maligned word, even though every society and group uses it freely to give hope as well as keep them in control.

The promise of heaven after death, land of milk and honey, the land of opportunity, the chosen people of God, infallibility of the senses, rationality of science, the superiority of the Nazi Aryans ... These are all examples of myths that people have followed throughout history. So, why can't we have a personal myth for ourselves, if it helps us in growth?

In fact, every successful person has a myth that they believe firmly. People like Alexander are glaring examples of it. The present-day management gurus say, 'Have a dream.' But that is not enough. If you truly want to go up, then have a myth.

Once you are convinced of what you can do, have firm faith in it, create a myth about you as 'the chosen one' or 'only you can do it,' and then go on. Your conviction will generate the turbo and your myth will push you forward.

The failed people never had a myth or faith in their uniqueness nor did they have enough power to move ahead. The two great dangers to one's growth are Scylla of lack of myth and Charybdis of empty imaginations. Steer clear of the two and you will marvel at your achievements.

A word of caution: the myth must be built around one's core strength, not around silly notions like 'I am unique' or that 'my love is unique.'

iii

Be a person of the future

Voltaire was a great French philosopher, thinker and writer. Will Durant, the great historian, was so impressed by Voltaire's life that he wrote, *The Story of Civilization,* to highlight his contribution. From the day I read his book, *Candid,* I have been a great admirer of Voltaire.

One of his stories that impressed me is *The Learned Brahmin.* It tells the story of a scholarly Brahmin who laments that, despite all his learning, he feels his life has been a waste and he has no peace. On the other hand, there is an elderly lady who does nothing, other than performing some basic rituals yet is at great peace. When told about her, the Brahmin said that under no condition would he exchange his inner turmoil for the peace as she was like an inert stone, with no chance of growth in this life.

A very powerful story, indeed.

In a similar story, a lazy woodcutter tells a hardworking woodcutter that he is already satisfied with life by working enough to meet his daily needs, so why would he work harder than the other one?

Such stories may draw laughter and smirks but also reveal how people get trapped into a state of inertness, resembling wood and stones. According to Indian thought, people are of three types: inert, active and calm. The inert kind, which is most of humanity, need to work hard to rise out of their fossilized state – India has been a burning example of this for thousands of years.

It is only the active types who have the

potential to grow in life. Innumerable books and talks help them increase their power further and give them direction. But that is not enough as one needs to be a person of the future.

Once, a friend of mine needed help in teaching Mathematics to his son. Since I had experience in that, I helped him by explaining things. Once the concepts were clear, the son shouted, 'God! It is all so simple! Why could I not understand all this in school?'

Indeed, why not? It is because the talented, master subjects in far less time than others. Consider scientists, authors or, most importantly, the prophets of any religion: they have always been ahead of their time. In fact, this is why the truly great become famous after their lifetime: 'a prophet is not worshipped in his own land.' Being ahead of their time, not many can appreciate them.

We may not be prophets or the pathfinders but we can always think ahead of time. Imagine how things would be and then work accordingly. I once knew one great monk who always thought at least fifty years ahead while building any building or a road in the ashram campus. Thinking ahead is not really difficult; in fact, most people who achieve greatness do it naturally.

One big problem is our inherent nature to accept the present as eternity. Due to this, when we are in sorrow, we think that we will not be able to laugh again. Jeffrey Archer, a noted popular author, was once jailed. He was so broken at the prison, he thought that he would not smile ever again. But as expected, once he was out of the confinement, his life got back on track.

I too have felt betrayed and concluded at times that I would never trust anyone again. But in no time, I found myself surrounded by my dependable friends. Even today, whenever I feel bogged down by some issue, I remind myself: 'Present is not eternity.'

The popular saying 'live in the present' is for the failed ones who have no desire to move forward. But those who wish to bloom, they must stop thinking that the present is everything and start imagining how things probably would be in the future and act accordingly.

Your work has to be for the future generation and never for those stuck in the present.

iv

Dignity in life, dignity in death

People have various perspectives on life and death, ranging from the ordinary to the divine. The Indian way of life, however, has a simple rule for all: 'dignity in life, dignity in death.'

When Swami Vivekananda visited America in 1893, in one of his speeches he told the audience, 'India taught the world how to die.' One young American commented, 'We know how to live.' Swamiji sternly replied, 'You know nothing.'

Indeed, this is the problem for most of us. Unless we learn how to die, how will we learn how to live? The present civilization, if we dare call it that, knows not how to live nor die. The rising disturbances around us prove the point.

How to die? In a dignified way, says India. This is illustrated in numerous stories and incidents of sacred books, such as the *Mahabharata,* written by the divine sage Vyasa in one lakh verses.

The *Mahabharata* is encyclopaedic in its stories and teachings about the art of living, including the dignity in death. One of its tales recounts how four divine *saranga* (a type of bird) fledglings were trapped in a forest fire. Their mother could not carry them away on her wings and the birdlings did not want her to die with them. When the mom suggested that the babies hide in the nearby rat hole, they refused, saying, 'It is better to die in the fire than to die ignominiously as a morsel for a rat.' In a twist of events, the fledglings prayed to Agni, who spared their lives.

Isn't it sad that most people have extremely undignified deaths?

A prayer in the Upanishads reveals how a devotee fully surrendered his mind to God at the time of death, praying, 'Now that I cannot move my limbs to offer my salutations to you, I mentally offer them.' My only wish in life is for a death where it will be only me and my *Ishta* (God) at the point of transition, with everything else fading away from my awareness.

Once the end is set, setting the course would not be difficult. It would be dignity regardless of victory, defeat, success or failure. This can be illustrated by a wonderful incident witnessed by Swami Vivekananda in Paris, 1895.

Once, while travelling by a horse carriage with his host, the coachman stopped the phaeton by a village road where a little boy and girl were walking with a maidservant. The coachman stepped down and caressed the children. Then he got back, took up the reins and proceeded along the road. With amazement, the host asked, 'Why did you do that? Those are a gentleman's children!' Turning in his seat, the coachman explained that he was once the manager of a large bank in Paris that had recently failed. With the little money that remained, he had bought the phaeton and horses to support his wife and children in a rented village house, with a maid who looked after them.

The calmness and dignity of the man deeply impressed Swamiji, who repeated this incident, 'This is what I call a Practical Vedantist. The man has understood the essence of Vedanta. Falling from such a high estate to this low condition, he is nonetheless unmoved. Thank God for such power of mind! This man is really a Vedantist!'

Vedanta, the religion of India, teaches one to maintain the calmness in mind regardless of success and failure, dignity in life and death.

In a similar story, when Alexander attacked the north-west frontiers of India and defeated King Porus, he asked how the king expected to be treated. To this, Porus replied, 'The way a king treats a king.'

When I had heard this story as a kid, it left a huge impression on me. Since then, I disliked people who lacked dignity. As a teacher, I always urged my students to hold their heads high in love, hatred, success or failure.

There were rare few occasions in my life when I was scorched by the flames of indignity and I regret them to this day.

Just like that, humility after success takes one forward, for victory and defeat, success and failure are parts of life's game. One never knows when we may collapse, so it is better not to be arrogant about our achievements.

Do not expect to rise in life if you do not stick to your dignity in victory or defeat, in life or death.

V

Trust your mentor

Some years ago, one of my former students contacted me as he became entangled in legal issues because of marital discord, a common phenomenon in India. He was getting in touch with me, after around twenty years. Somehow, he had felt that I could help him out of the mess.

As for the legal issue, I could do nothing, but his mental state needed medical intervention. He himself was an M.D. doctor, so when I suggested that he right away consult a doctor, he strongly resisted, insisting that drugs were of no use and that, being a doctor, he knew this better than I.

After a few days, I read in the papers that he could not face the ignominy of arrests and had committed suicide. It would be impolite of me to say that medicines could have saved him.

Gita, one of the foremost sacred books of India, begins with a beautiful narration of Arjuna, a great warrior, overcoming the confusion about right and wrong as he partook in the *dharma yuddha* (righteous war) against his own kin.

Having exhausted his decision-making

power, he told his friend-mentor Lord Krishna, 'Overpowered by confusion and emotions, I pray to you, as a disciple who has taken refuge in you, to tell me what to do.' (Gita: II.7) Sri Krishna narrated the philosophy of life, duty, dignity, etc. and said to Arjuna, 'You now decide what you want to do.'

Our decision-making is shaped by four factors: learnings from parents, teachers, friends and one's own conscience. Once our decision-making process has collapsed, we must turn to our mentor and then do exactly what is being suggested, instead of applying our vitiated understanding.

To be clear, a mentor in life need not be only one person. One may have quite a few trusted guides who help when in a confusion or in a crisis.

One serious problem with the seekers of help is that they do not truly wish to listen to guidance. Instead, they try to impose their own ideas and want those ratified! That, of course, is a sure path to doom, rather than growth and glory.

6

Acts Are Eloquent

The uniqueness of a living being lies in its ability to act. In a broader sense, there is never a moment when a being is not active. Even when we are acting inert, our mind is conscious of the fact that we are not doing anything.

Our acts are of three kinds: mental, verbal and physical. It is through these that we learn and also express ourselves, implying that our evolution and falling back depend entirely on our acts.

One important aspect of action is moral authority, born of noble acts and character, is far more powerful than mere authority. To lose moral authority means to lose control over those who are under our charge.

This section gives a perspective on the most visible aspect of our personality: our actions. A senior monk used to say that our actions should be good and they should also look good. Even when we help others, every act should be in sync with our values.

i

Our acts are our brand ambassadors

Our acts are our brand ambassadors; sometimes they push our reputation, noble or otherwise, far ahead of us.

The acts we perform can be categorized as meaningful, lazy, scattered, frittered and meaningless. There is the story of a mentally unsound man who used to go out every morning breaking the thrown-away earthen pots (a common practice in India until some years ago) and would complain each evening about how he had to work so much every day! Unfortunately, that is something most of us do daily.

To move upward in life, our acts need to be in line with our chosen way of life, known as *dharma.* Nothing should move a person away from that. A fascinating story from Valmiki's *Ramayana* is when Sri Rama reached the ocean shore in search of Sita. His army was disheartened by the sheer distance between the ocean and Lanka, where Ravana had taken Sita.

Sri Rama prayed to the ocean god and fasted for three days but got no response. Angered, Sri Rama picked up his divine bow and arrow and threatened to dry up the ocean. The ocean god then appeared and said, 'I cannot give up my *dharma* out of fear or greed! So, I cannot give way to you just like that. However, you can make a bridge on the ocean to cross over.' This bridge later came to be known as *Rama Setu.*

We often fail because we cross the defining boundaries of our duty and way of life. Once it is crossed, the inimical forces find our vulnerability and attack us.

Does that mean that noble people do not fail or suffer? They do but the strength born of character makes them rise from the ashes. After all, India does not see life as a one-time chance but as an ongoing chain through births.

Even if one does not believe in rebirth, the satisfaction of staying true to one's conviction is always phenomenal and its effects are felt by the next generation.

Stay true to yourself, then there can be no failure for you.

ii

Destiny is for the lazy; destination is for the horses

Since our childhood, we are trained to reach the next milestone. Those who are good at reaching the posts are declared as achievers.

While this may seem innocent, this kind

of orientation is shaped by the erroneous philosophy of life we learn from our surroundings and then get used to it. The materialistic outlook creates an impression that 'you live only once.'

In addition, some religions believe that God created this universe as a one-time affair. God being God, there must be a purpose to His act of creation; therefore, we too must have a goal in life along with the belief that God must have destined something for us.

Newtonian physics looks at the universe as a huge machine which God has set into motion. So, we all must be cogs, big or small and hence, must have a purpose and destiny. Darwin's theory of evolution, too, implies that we must evolve towards being some kind of 'superman,' as also popularized by Nietzsche in his work, *Thus Spoke Zarathustra.*

But no, according to the Indian view, there is never a destination. The masters of spirituality have shown repeatedly that whatever world we might be in, including heaven, we are always on the move. If we can attain the knowledge of spiritual oneness, then we can go beyond the world. The conclusion is that there never is any destination! We are the meaning and purpose of existence.

Indeed, goals are for the horses and destination is for the lazy. The truly successful see milestones as passing sights on one's way of life.

iii

Inconsistency implies lack of importance

Patanjali's Yoga Sutras is the most important book on how to be a yogi. It is written in the style of aphorisms (short phrases) that detail everything about the mind, its constitution, ways to control it and the pitfalls faced while doing so.

One of the *sutras* says that a person needs to practice with full intensity and respect for a very long period, the success depends on the level of efforts.

What is true of yoga is also true in everyday life. People want to move upward but they neither have consistency, nor respect, nor the sense of urgency. Most failures are rooted in one's inconsistency which shows that the act is not important for them. If a person is consistent for a long time in one area, their failings are bound to stop.

Sri Ramakrishna narrated the story of two farmers who dug a canal to bring river water to their farms. Both started their work with diligence. At noon, one farmer obeyed his wife's call for food and rest. But the other one became furious, when asked to do the same. He continued digging the canal until water started flowing in the evening. Only then did he stop to bathe and eat.

Inconsistency shows lack of passion and hence, lack of importance. If something is important for us, we will then do it at any hour of the day, as a mother cares for her baby.

If we are inconsistent about what we do, then either we need to change our habits or know that it is not meant for us.

Also, patchwork solutions do not work when a person is not serious about their acts. When Arjuna was in epic dilemma regarding the *Kurukshetra* war, Lord Sri Krishna did not offer him any patchwork solution. Instead, he explained to Arjuna the philosophy of life and suggested that his acts should be in consonance with his way of life which was to be a valiant warrior.

iv

Never do something that will make your enemies happy

The great epic *Mahabharata* is like a treasure house of stories that teach how to live a dignified life. One of its lesser known but powerful stories is that of Vidula and her son who was the crown prince of his land.

Once, the kingdom of Vidula was attacked by powerful enemies. In the deadly war, the prince nearly got defeated and ran away to save his life from the battlefield, straight to his room.

Vidula questioned his behaviour: how he could behave in such a cowardly fashion? The prince narrated the war and said that as a mother, Vidula should be happy that he could save his life.

As a Kshatriya princess, Vidula screamed at him and said that she would love to see her son die on the battlefield than see him turn into a coward. During the conversation, she famously said, 'Your acts are making your enemies laugh at you. Go back to the battlefield.'

Such inspiring words!

Sri Krishna had also said similar words to Arjuna when he had become weak, 'Your enemies will say unspeakable words about your valour. What can be worse for a warrior like you?' He further added, 'It is better for the respectable to die than to face dishonour.'

When our acts are ignoble and our failures become eloquent, we not only give our critics and enemies a chance to laugh at us but also make our dear ones suffer the ignominy which gets carried forward from generation to generation.

V

Counter stigma through glorious deeds

Try howsoever we may, things can go wrong and may make us look weak, helpless or an object of ridicule. There is no way that one can get rid of stigma but it is possible to counter that by performing glorious deeds.

In *Ramayana* by Valmiki, when Sita, the divine consort of Sri Rama, was abducted by Ravana who claimed that since Sita was living in his part of the kingdom, it was within his rights to take her away.

Sri Rama, a Kshatriya prince, refused to accept his reason. He gathered an army, attacked Lanka and killed Ravana in the fierce battle that ensued. He admitted that there was a blemish on his valour when his wife was abducted. But now, by killing his enemy, he had washed it away with his prowess.

We now remember Sri Rama for the strength that he showed and not that his wife got abducted.

This is an important aspect of failing upward: we will be remembered for our great works and not for our failings. The strength of a chain is measured by its weakest link but a tree is known by its best fruits and not by the worm-eaten, rotten ones. Even great authors and poets have ordinary works in their name but are known and respected for their best ones.

Of course, there will always be serial fault finders ... But who cares for them?

vi

No revenge, please

The great author and thinker, Leo Tolstoy describes the dangers of revenge in his famous story *Quench the Spark*. Two families were friendly neighbours. Unfortunately, a quarrel over an egg ensued when the hen of one family laid the egg in the yard of the other. From an initial verbal conflict, it escalated to a feud between the two families which continued for years. Even children lived with the enmity and the idea of revenge. Finally, one issue reached the court with nasty consequences.

In the Indian tradition, there are innumerable stories with revengeful tendencies that had nasty consequences.

According to the Buddhist traditions, Milarepa is a prominent monk in Tibetan Buddhism. During his childhood, he and his mother suffered from the hands of their relatives. His mother, filled with bitterness, sent Milarepa to learn black magic. When he returned with the powers, he unleashed them on his relatives. Many burnt to death because of his rash and revengeful act. Later, he regretted his actions and left his mother to become a monk and suffer in silence.

In our daily life, we find children and people showing off their superiority, for which they may even indulge in vengeful acts. As a reminder, Sri Rama was not in revenge mode against Ravana; rather he had given his enemy many chances to return Sita.

Anyone wishing to go upward in life must get rid of acts that are powered by the forces of revenge. Anger, the mother of all vengeful acts, has the deadly habit of burning the beholder of the blame rather than whom the flame is directed.

7

Strength

Aldous Huxley describes a character in his novel, *Point Counterpoint,* who laments, towards the end of his life, that he wasted it by walking when he was meant to fly. A very powerful statement, particularly because most of us do not know what we are meant for; we do not know what our true strength is.

This section shares ideas on this all-important topic, since most of us fail because we lack strength.

i

Know your strength

It is difficult to devise a system that can accurately predict one's strength but there are broad indicators that can help us discover our core. It is also important to understand that, except for the super-achievers, the area of strength for most people keeps changing because they are not truly good at something in exclusion of others.

Broadly speaking, what one is afraid to lose is their core strength. A good sportsperson may compromise in some areas but not in their field of play. If God were to ask us which one quality we would like to keep, the answer that comes first to mind is usually our strength.

There are other markers for one's core strength:

1. We do not copy others in our area of strength. For example, no great cricketer ever copies the style of another cricketer and no two great writers are alike. Strength

means maintaining individuality amid all odds.

2. The activity that one can perform smoothly and effortlessly is their strength.
3. Strength is when one focuses only on the act, irrespective of praise or criticism. Albert Spalding, one of the USA's great instrumentalists in the twentieth century, was once upset about a negative newspaper review. He was scolded by another great musician with, 'I thought you were a musician.' It meant that if he were true to his art then he would never pay attention to what others said about his performance. He wrote in his memoir that from then on, he never read any reviews of his performances.
4. Arrogance is a sign of weakness. True strength always makes a person humble, since it gives them the strength to hold on to their strength. Thus, a strong person does not show off. A martial arts expert does not throw kicks at anyone when angry; they reserve them for their special fights only.

5. We love doing what our core strength is and thus, do not get tired of it easily. We may feel physical fatigue but work again. On the other hand, we get easily tired when it is not our core area.

I knew a gentleman who loved painting so deeply that he would do so through the night, with no thoughts of hunger and sleep.

There can be many other tests. We only have to know what we are truly good at and then focus on it without a care for fame or blame.

One interesting thing that I have observed about strong people is that they are all invariably very simple. They are neither complex in their mindset, nor do they understand others' complexities. Here, simplicity does not mean stupidity. They are intelligent, capable, experts in their fields and yet non-complex.

ii

Gather the spread to gain strength

Most people feel that they have no qualities, i.e., they lack strength. What to do about it?

A serious problem in life is the 'one life theory,' which makes people rush through things. When they fail to excel, they begin scraping and scratching at whatever they can find. In the process, they lose even their peace.

As young students, we followed the routine where each class period lasted around forty minutes. Following the same pattern, we often made a daily routine for ourselves. These schedules collapsed in a day during the holidays, much like our New Year's resolutions. Premchand, a great Hindi writer, wrote a beautiful story, full of fun and satire, titled *Bade Bhai Sahab.* The protagonist made a routine for himself but it always collapsed within a day.

A senior monk once told me: 'Routine is good for those who are totally scattered, but if you want to grow, you have to work on a single project for long hours, for long years.' This is true for any study, research and meditation, too.

A serious problem is the 'spread' of our attention, extending from household affairs, through sports, politics, world affairs and finally to our own work.

Time and tranquillity are our only assets in life. So, if these two are spread too thin in what we are doing, then we can never have the strength to succeed. In the *Mahabharata,* there is the story of Bhim, who went to the kitchen during the night for extra food. One day, Arjuna caught him and asked why he was eating in the dark. Bhim replied that since he knew where the mouth was, darkness was no deterrent. This gave Arjuna the idea to practise archery in the dark. With sustained practice, he became the greatest warrior of his time.

There are many amazing stories and incidents from the lives of every great achiever about how they gathered their strength into one single goal before they succeeded.

It may not be possible to withdraw from the unnecessary overnight but we must start cutting down right away. In fact, we will be surprised to learn what we can do without in life.

Try making a list of such useless things to have a hearty laugh.

iii

Need for pattern in life

One potent way to build up strength is to have a pattern in life, one that focuses on one's purpose.

Some years ago, an old sadhu at Rishikesh used to come every morning for Ganga *darshan.* Once, he fell ill and managed to drag himself to the banks with the support of two juniors. One of our senior monks there requested, 'Swamiji, you can wait for a few days and come again when you are well and fit.'

The elderly sadhu furiously said, 'You mean to say that I should give more value to my mortal body than coming to pay my *pranams* to the divine mother Ganga? What kind of a monk are you?'

Those unfamiliar with the life of monks and sadhus should know that we are trained to pay less importance to our body and the world in comparison to spiritual connection.

Our senior monk was so impressed that he often repeated it to stress the importance of regularity and pattern for growth in life.

Parents often say that their child has huge potential but somehow failed. If probed further, the invariable reason would be a lack of consistency and pattern in life.

One need not make a minute-to-minute routine to regulate life but having a broad pattern is very important. I have been lucky to have seniors in my life who insisted on its importance and made sure that I did that!

iv

Have a quality that will make people come to you again

Once, I was travelling by train with a young couple as my co-passengers. During our conversation, they asked me, 'What do you do?'

'I am a monk,' I said, implying that being a monk is the ultimate Indian tradition.

'Yes, that is fine. But what do you do?' asked the young lady. Being from the new generation, it was beyond her comprehension that being a monk is a way of life. So, to calm her curiosity, I said that I teach and I also write books. 'Oh!' said she, 'I've never heard the name.' And that was the end of it.

Deep down, it was a very interesting conversation. You may be a government officer, doctor, engineer, etc., but for a person to recognize your value, you must have a quality you excel in. You must excel in something that would make others come to you repeatedly.

In a similar incident, two college girls, emotional with broken hearts, came to meet me. In a few minutes, I realized that they were as empty as emptiness could be. So, I said, 'Tell me, sisters, why would your friends come back to you for a second time? Do you have any qualities that would make them stick to you?' They got upset with me and left.

Most people have this entitlement. They feel that others have to give them respect and value for simply being what they are. But the reality is that unless we have something special in us, we will be treated as a vendor who sells only stale products.

Once we realize our special zing, we also stop seeking attention from others.

V

Have additional skills; have a hobby

The rapid growth of technology and the consequent advancement in society have made things obsolete, so much so that people have ended up losing their profession and thus, making them dependent on government doles and social charities. This makes them feel unwanted and depressed.

Having grown up in an Indian village, I have seen good bullock cart drivers and ploughmen lose everything when new technology took over. Some years ago, the community of bird catchers, known as *baheliya*, protested at many places because of the ban on bird catching.

The sense of worthlessness born out of such situations can be devastating.

The lucky ones sometimes get big packages for voluntary retirement, after which they start looking for *babajis* who can keep them engaged through their frothy talks and maybe with some voluntary activities.

To have a meaningful life, it is important to be very good at some skill and, along with it, reasonably good at some other unrelated skill. The human mind is so powerful that it can easily let us acquire two skills. For example,

John von Neumann, a celebrated physicist, developed Game Theory, which later helped John Nash win the Nobel Prize in Economics.

Einstein was good enough at violin to give lessons to a young man at a party. In fact, most talented people are very good at more than one skill.

More importantly, one must have an impersonal hobby. This helps in clearing the cobwebs of the mind and thus makes a person fit to be better at what they do. Even if they are forced into retirement, at least they will have something to fiddle with, as Nero is supposed to have done when Rome was burning!

vi

To give is to grow

The weak crave love but the strong love to love. The weak cling but the strong give all. The weak scream of revenge but the strong forgive; the weak are possessive but the strong give freedom.

The common human failings like lust, greed, anger, jealousy, misery and expectation, are all rooted in human frailty. It is the weak who have the luxury to indulge in such emotions; the strong stay away from emotions.

In the Indian way of life, the correctness of an action is judged by the oneness of the action and its result. The technical expression for this is *Phalarupta*. For example, the result of devotion to God is devotion and the result of love is love. So, if we want to succeed after many failures, we need to look at end result and then practise the same. So, if a weak person wants to become strong, they have to learn to give, forgive and love instead of asking, vengeance and begging to be loved.

Even the blame game, in which people often indulge, is rooted in holding back because of weakness. In my youth, I always blamed someone else for every problem, unaware that it could be my mistake. I was not mature enough to realize that I was the cause of my own chaos. Now I know better.

The simple principle of growth, after all the failings, is 'give to grow.' It can never let anyone down.

vii

Value your life; society has invested in you

Many decades ago, I had read the condensed version of the book *Alive: The Story of the Andes Survivors* by Piers Paul Read, about the survivors of Uruguayan Air Force Flight 571 that crashed in 1972.

The chartered flight, carrying forty-five people, a rugby team along with their friends and family, crashed in a remote mountain from where escape was nearly impossible. When their food stock was exhausted, people started dying one after another. Thus, they had to start eating the flesh of the dead who had been so dear to them only a few days ago!

One member was offered all the food so he could trek and look for help. But at the last minute, he refused (I am narrating it from my memory, so details may vary a bit). The other survivors condemned him, 'We sacrificed our food to give you strength, now you cannot back out.' Finally, he went and the remaining sixteen of them were rescued.

The incident left a deep impression on me about the importance of giving back to society. We need to understand the importance of building up our strength, for society has invested so much in us: time, energy, emotions, wealth … Everything.

This should awaken our dormant sense of responsibility and consequently, pull us up and move. The ideas like 'my life, my choice' and 'I am free to do what I want to do' are a social betrayal.

viii

Latke raho: Hold on

One phrase that has helped me hold on to growth has been '*Latke Raho*: Keep holding on.'

A dear friend in the national police force once told me of his early days at the police academy. He narrated how he was selected to be an officer due to his weight and sent to the academy for training. He had never exercised in life nor had he played outdoor games, so going through the bone-breaking exercises was too much for him.

Once, during a session of rope climbing, he somehow climbed up to a height and looking down from there, let go of the rope with the hope that he would break his leg and be expelled from the academy.

His experienced drill sergeant must have faced such cases in the past, so upon seeing him contemplating self-inflicted injury, he shouted at him, '*Latke raho, sahab* (Keep holding onto the rope); even that will build your muscle strength.' The gentleman persevered and his life changed forever. Before he retired, he was the Director General of a police force.

Whenever I felt low, I recounted this story and told myself, 'Indeed, *latke raho*. Even that will build muscles.' Climbing up is not always a test of growth; even holding on is some kind of growth. Whatever one's profession or station of life, one must learn to hold on.

ix

The ultimate strength

Whenever I read about the sacrifices of people made for their nation, ideals or religion, I always marvel at the power in their minds that they willingly laid down their lives. The world has seen enough of crusades, jihads and suicide bombings to know the power of conviction based on lies and half-truths. Just as the people of Israel have survived persecution for thousands of years simply by believing that they are the chosen people, suicide bombers have believed that the gates of heaven are open for them.

When self-help writers write, 'you can do' or 'you can win,' many are convinced and attempt to uplift themselves. So, massive power can come from a simple spiritual truth, 'we are divine!' It is beyond our imagination to feel the gush of strength if one gets even a little of this conviction. What would happen if we were convinced of the divine connection within us?

India has preached that we are neither 'sinners' nor 'fallen' but fully and wholly divine: 'Divinity is our birthright.' No one can harm me until I let them; I am the eternal king, so why should I beg from anyone? I am eternal, so why should I ever hurry like a pauper? I am divine, so why should I crave for anything? The list goes on.

Yes, we are divine, the children of the Divine and see the volcanic eruption of strength within us!

8

Weakness

From the time that Abrahamic religions and Western culture began to sway over the Indian mindset, we started learning the ideas of weakness and temptation as something black and deadly, personified as Satan and the Devil, prowling to eat up the naive.

Weakness causes failure, so it is important to understand its dynamics.

One simple way of understanding weakness is this: if someone takes us lightly, mocks or humiliates us, it shows we are weak in the area where they are strong. This does not include the criticism by the uncultured or the upstarts.

i

Weakness is the sign of awakening

As a young monk, I was recommended to read *Thais*, a famous novel by Anatole France. It is a simple story of an ascetic hermit who is swayed by Thais, a libertine beauty. Under the sway of passion, he poses as her redeemer and forces her to join a convent, where she becomes devout. The hermit, as if possessed by the devil, sinks down and down.

It was a disturbing story and filled me with irrational fears, for India does not believe in permanent fall. When a society believes that life is limited, hurrying becomes an obvious corollary. People either dive headlong into looting as much as they can from the world or they start whipping themselves into their beliefs, however silly those might be.

In contrast, India treats existence as eternal, so only the foolish would get into the acceleration mode. More importantly, we do not accept weakness, sin or temptation as inherent or even iron-clad. We are not 'born sinners,' not even when born by mistake; we are here by choice and we live the life we believe to be the best for us.

What is the weakness, then? And temptation?

Weakness, temptation, sin, mistake – call it by any name – is the sign of awakening of what we have inside. We have to decide whether we want to continue with it or outgrow it. When the sage Viswamitra, previously mentioned, succumbed to anger, revenge and then to lust for Menaka, each 'fall' was a reminder, sometimes gentle and at other times harsh, that he had inside him.

Once we realize that a trait exists in us, we can either live with it or give it up, depending on what we want from life. Viswamitra wanted to become a sage, so he gave up the divine Menaka and their newborn Shakuntala. That is how we received the most important mantra from the Vedas, *Gayatri*.

Bhagwan Buddha wanted to discover the root cause of misery. He left his wife and newborn son. Thus, we have the religion of peace, Buddhism.

On the other hand, we have kings like Sri Rama and Janaka, a kingmaker like Sri Krishna, a scholar like Yajnavalkya and a weaver like Kabir, all spiritually accomplished even though they were married and led the life of householders.

Once we become aware of our desires, we need to train our mind to accept the 'fight or flight' approach. If this does not work, we need to learn to live with it and perform great deeds. In the long run, our weaknesses may be the fodder for the critics and authors, but people will remember us for the great things that we did.

To give an example, Stephen Hawking suffered from serious disabilities. Today, he is remembered for his contributions in mathematical physics and not his limitations. Just like that, weaknesses are mere limitations.

ii

Repeated falls

Once, an elderly shoe-lifter was caught outside the temple at Belur Math, where I live. The thief was well-dressed and his speech polished. Amused, I asked him why he indulged in such acts. He replied sheepishly in a soft voice, '*Aar korbo na*' (I won't do it again). I laughed and laughed and I am still smiling while writing. He reminded me of kids at our residential school who, when caught committing mischief, always swore the same thing and would get caught again within a few days.

In a similar incident, we had a very nice student from a noble, rich family who loved to steal pens. In his zest for his odd mania, he spared neither the teachers, nor the principal, nor the hostel superintendents. One day, when he was finally caught by one student, it was found that he literally used to sleep on a bed of pens!

This incident happened many years ago. But even at that time, I was amazed at his proficiency and wondered how many births it must have taken him to be a perfect kleptomaniac!

There is a popular term, 'serial offender' that signifies a state of loose morality that results in repeated lapses. While the term may be useful in penal and legal parlance, it has no value in the Indian way of life. Failure, weakness, temptation, etc., are reminders that in our past life we were adept at it! So, why lament over what we could have been good at in our previous births!

However, if we want to get out of a particular vice that is hardwired in us, we will have to take countermeasures for a very long time. Be ready for the long haul and have patience until then.

iii

Convert weakness into strength

Raskhan, one of the great Hindi poets devoted to Sri Krishna, was formerly known as Syed Ibrahim Khan and grew up in opulence.

According to a popular story, he was infatuated with a Hindu boy. One day, a Vaishnava saint told him, 'If you loved Krishna the way you love the boy, you would find salvation.' Ibrahim did not look back after that and went away to Vrindavan forever, where he devoted himself to Sri Krishna. His passion for the ordinary had now matured into love for God.

In a strikingly similar story, Tulsidas was madly in love with his wife. When ridiculed about his passion, he changed overnight into a great poet of devotion and wrote the famous *Ramcharitmanas*.

Likewise, once a boy was caught sending letters to a girl, it was a serious taboo during that time. When informed, the son's father said aloud, 'God! My son now knows such beautiful English! What expression!' The boy grew up to be a good writer.

The story of *Ben-Hur* by Lew Wallace is quite popular and fascinating. Ben-Hur was a Jew who was tragically and illegally sold as a slave to the Romans. In those days, ships were manned by slaves who were often whipped to act faster. When the owner of the ship asked how Ben-Hur was faring, he was informed that the only favour he wanted was to be allowed to sit alternately on both sides of the ship while rowing. When asked to explain the reason, Ben-Hur said that he wanted the muscles of both his arms to become equally strong.

This story has been a lifelong lesson for me: Whenever in crisis, make the best use of the little opportunity that might exist. As I grew, I found that this has been the practice of every great personality. Al Ghazali, a great scholar, spent his time in meditation whenever he was in jail, which was often and also collected books and studied them whenever he got out.

In fact, there is nothing called weakness or fall or failing; it is all perspective. A young adult who falls in love repeatedly has within him the capacity to love the entire humanity. A good liar can be a great actor and spymaster. Those who have suffered can be great peacemakers. Those who are excessively active can serve society very well. The list goes on.

If someone criticizes us for some personality fault, we need to decide whether we want to live with that or convert it into our strong point. It is not at all difficult.

iv

Focus on strength, not on weakness

One of the very fascinating stories in the *Mahabharata* is when the Pandavas left their kingdom and went to the Himalayas in the hope of attaining heaven.

The five brothers, Yudhisthira, Bhim, Arjuna, Nakul and Sahadeva, had a common wife, Draupadi. They had a big battle with their cousins, the Kauravas, who were killed in the war. Though victorious, they felt remorse over the killings and after some years, they set on their last journey, the *mahaprasthan.*

Yudhisthira was leading the way. On the way, Draupadi was the first to fall, then Sahadeva, Nakul, Arjuna and finally, Bhim. As each one of them fell, Yudhisthira kept commenting on their weakness: Draupadi was partial in her love towards Arjuna; Sahadeva thought that he was the wisest person; Nakul considered himself handsome; Arjuna bragged; Bhim was gluttonous.

So, why did Yudhisthira never mention the faults to them, even though he was the eldest and the leader? Simply because we all have some intrinsic faults that can never be corrected! If he had mentioned the shortcomings, there would have been heartburn and ill will, without any considerable gain.

This is how you handle life. Keep your weakness within permissible limits and focus on your strength.

We can keep working on our weaknesses and failings, but nothing will come of it. But if we focus on our strength, consolidate and enhance it, then we can achieve anything. We will be remembered for our strength; only the critics will focus on our weakness.

Interestingly, Indian scriptures do not ask us to be perfect, unlike Abrahamic religions. Indian sacred books say: 'Know yourself.' That will burn down all your Karma, good and bad. It simply means that our weakness will not obstruct our path of spirituality, as long as we can focus fully on the Divine. After that, the weakness will become like fried seeds, incapable of causing damage.

9

Attacks and Crisis

i

Why shouldn't good people suffer?

A famous song by Surdas, a great poet-saint of India who was blind since childhood, says: '*Murakha-murakha raje kinhe pandit phirata bhikhaari*' (Strange are the ways of Karma; it makes the wise poor and the foolish rich).

Like most people, I too admired this line and used it to assert how much injustice there is in this world and why good people must suffer in the hands of the cruel, etc.

But why should it be otherwise? If good

people die, suffer diseases, mosquito bites, hunger or thirst, then why shouldn't they too suffer like everyone else?

At the root of the misconception that good people should not suffer is the philosophy of spiritual materialism. According to this, some people preach and believe that God saves his devotees and hence would protect them from harm. When extended further, it implies that good people should not suffer!

And yet, there is absolutely no rhyme or reason behind this. Good and honest people, too, have to suffer as much as others. There is no rationale or justification to prove otherwise.

Even those who believe God is the giver of good and bad need to understand that He cannot be partial towards anyone, neither to His devotees nor to the noble and good. God gives something to us all; He gives the lions the power to kill and He gives deer powerful legs to run; He gives poison to the snakes and anti-venom to the doctors; wisdom to some and riches to others; goodness to some and power to others. No one can have a claim over what is God's, for we are all His children.

Moreover, a person is good simply because their nature won't allow them to act otherwise and a bad one is so for the same reason. The qualities have been perfected over births! An honest person will not leave their honesty under normal conditions and a chaste person will never indulge in extramarital affairs even if they get such an opportunity or are under some pressure. The satisfaction from having a quality itself is the result of goodness. So, the hope of encashing it for something else is plain mischief or ignorance.

A wise person knows that attacks and crises can come at any time, like death, disease or even disaster, so they never collapse when something happens. It is only the fragile ones who blame God for their sorry plight.

The question to ask oneself shouldn't be 'why me?' but 'why not me?'

ii

We invited it upon ourselves

Who should be blamed for attacks and crises that we may face in life? The simplistic answers may range from God, fate, Karma, chance, etc. However, deep down, we make ourselves vulnerable and let crisis hit us. The viruses and bacteria attack us all the time but we succumb to them only when our immune system is down.

A strong house can withstand floods, tornadoes and cyclones; it is the thatched houses that get blown away.

I once knew an honest government officer who was falsely implicated by his detractors. I felt bad for him, yet I also felt that he had let his guard down, which made him vulnerable.

A very interesting story from the *Puranas* highlights this truth. The divine lady Diti longed for an unconquerable son. Her husband, the great sage Kashyap, blessed her and asked her to follow certain rituals.

Indra, the king of the gods was the son of Diti's sister and the sage Kashyap. Being the king of the heavens, it was his responsibility to maintain order in the universe. Hearing about Diti's vows, he felt that her child would create an imbalance of power, so he was on the lookout to destroy the child in the womb but because of the rituals Diti did, he could not succeed.

One night, Diti was feeling tired, so she did not wash her feet before sleeping. That loophole was all Indra was looking for. Through that small chink, he entered Diti's womb and cut the baby into pieces. Since the baby was immortal because of the father's blessings, so Indra cut the child into forty-nine pieces. These immortal pieces became the forty-nine winds: *Maruts*. Thus, Diti could not have a baby who could surpass Indra in valour because of the little lapse.

When surrounded by inimical forces, it is necessary to make ourselves foolproof; otherwise, there will always be a security breach.

In *Ramayana*, we find that Sita was abducted by Ravana for no fault of hers and was kept in captivity for nearly a year. When Sri Rama killed Ravana in the war that ensued, Sita was rescued. Later, Sri Rama commented that he knew all along that Sita's innate chastity would protect her from the lustful intents of Ravana, which was indeed true.

Whenever devastation takes place due to a security breach, the best thing for us to do is to collect the remaining pieces and start rebuilding life again. What would follow may be better or worse but the rebuilding must be done.

iii

Save yourself from your own power

While the problem born out of external attacks always exists, especially for the honest and noble people, a more dangerous crisis comes to people with an excess of power that may cause self-explosion.

I have seen quite a few cases where someone with excess power indulged in acts that ended up harming them. In a tragic story from the *Ramayana*, King Dasaratha, the father of Sri Rama, was so good at archery that he could hit a target in darkness, too. Empowered by his skill, he often went for night hunting. Unfortunately, he once killed a sagely young man, Shravan Kumar, who had gone to take water from a pond for his blind parents, whom he was taking on a pilgrimage. When the parents heard the news, they cursed the king that he too would die of grief over his lost son.

When a burning matchstick does not get fuel, it burns itself.

The Sanskrit word for power is *rajas*. When there is an excess of *rajas*, one behaves like an animal whose tail is on fire; they want to conquer the world and feel that they can do anything. In most cases, they end up harming themselves. So, it is always a good idea to have innocent habits and practices that would keep such people engaged to vent out the excess in them.

iv

Constant attacks mean that we are growing

I know people who complained of facing non-stop attacks and criticisms, often for no fault of theirs. Initially, I did not know what to tell them but with time, I realized that it simply means that you are too powerful or you are growing in power.

In India, probably all over the world, the quarrel between a daughter-in-law and the mother-in-law has been infamous, often ending with nasty consequences. What people often fail to realize is that all these quarrels are because a new member of the family is growing in power, which would soon challenge the erstwhile powerful. There is no other reason for it.

My favourite example to explain spirituality and worldly power is that of swimming in the Ganga. It has been dear and sacred to me like a mother. If someone is swimming with the current, they can create a favourable setup by pulling the good things and pushing away the dirty, like a carcass.

However, when one starts swimming against the flow, like going from Kolkata to Haridwar, then they will have no choice but to create favourable conditions. Starting from the force of the flow to getting hit by the unwanted – these will continue throughout the journey.

If everything is going smoothly in life, it simply means we are not moving upward. Going down with the stream requires no labour, no pains; it is the upward movement that invites ridicule, criticism and attacks. More of these mean that we are moving up more and more.

V

Darkness before dawn

Crisis and failings are not only the gateway to new opportunities but also quite normal before a big event. It is difficult to say why it happens but it happens.

In spiritual life, temptations invariably come and seem to derail one's life. Many saints have also reported that they developed deep doubts about God just before their realization.

In an occurrence when Swami Vivekananda went to Chicago in 1893 to take part in the World Parliament of Religions, where he represented Hindu Dharma, he faced innumerable setbacks and crises. He was left with no money, no acquaintances, no place to stay, unfriendly people, etc. Think of a problem and he had to face it. He desperately asked his well-wishers in India to send him money so he could come back! Finally, he reached the stage where he uttered the now-famous five words, 'Sisters and Brothers of America,' which marked the beginning of a new era in the world of religions.

There is a famous expression in Sanskrit, '*Shreyanshi bahu vighnani*' (every noble act has to face many obstacles). Of these, the darkness before dawn is the most powerful one.

10

People and Company

By our inherent nature and training, we like to be social and in some cases, we get close to those with whom we have compatibility. Unfortunately, some of them hurt us and even harm us. How should we handle all this?

i

When loved ones leave

Imagine a beautiful garden, created and nurtured by us. Think of it as having some huge trees, while others are large or small. One day, a storm hits it and uproots some majestic trees, leaving the smaller saplings intact. What can we do then? Nothing. We can only shed tears at our loss. Worse, we may outgrow our loss but the pits of the large trees would always remind us of what we lost.

Rejection in life is exactly like that. To nurture relationships, we pour our sweat and blood, invest our time and emotions, forget our own selves and at some point in time, we meet with loss in the form of someone walking away from our lives. Even when we let go of the loss, the craters of emotions left behind can never be filled.

Trauma caused by such losses can hurt the sensitive pretty hard. However, having seen and experienced life quite closely, I have realized that:

1. Being alone is better than having fake relationships. We are often trapped in emotional bonds that only sap away our individuality.
2. People who leave you did not deserve you.

They were the leeches who had their drink and then fell away.

3. When the so-called loved ones start ridiculing or abusing us, it means that the stretch of our togetherness is over.

Here, we are not discussing losses due to death or disease but the loss that one experiences when someone goes away from life on their own, citing some reason or no reason at all.

Srimad Bhagavatam, a sacred text of India, poetically describes loss and suffering (X.47.6-8):

> A relation (by those who are not relatives) is made only for achieving a purpose and it lasts only till the purpose is completed, as in the case of love shown by men to women and bees to flowers. Courtesans leave the poor lover, people leave an incompetent king, students leave their teachers after receiving the degree, priests leave after they get their

fees during a yajna, birds leave a tree after its fruits are exhausted, guests leave the host after finishing their meals, beasts leave a forest that is burnt down and a paramour after enjoying the women though attached to him.

So, there is no reason to feel dejected when people leave us. As the above quotation implies, it is in the nature of beings to move on once they have nothing more to gain by being with us. It does not show our incompetence; rather, in most cases, they may be like a small pot getting overfilled by a large tanker.

ii

Don't tango with those who take away your individuality

There is a popular story in India about a crow that was impressed with the flight style of a swan, full of grace, unlike other birds. The crow started imitating the swan but without any success. And, having copied the swan's style for long, it even forgot how to fly like a crow.

As kids, we have our idols and stars whom we want to imitate. However, compared to the animals, we are not the herd types, since we are all unique and have individuality that must not be compromised. Imitating and copying must be left for children.

Unfortunately for us, when we are in a company, particularly the wrong one, we tend to lose our individuality because we want to be like them. Worse, we lose our self-esteem and self-respect, which may prove to be disastrous in the long run and may even cause health hazards.

It is important to wake up to one's individuality and stay away from people who seem to take away that. Many people lose their chance of growth simply because they were under the influence of people who took away their individuality. This happens more intensely in friendship, love, idolization and in organized workplaces. One must learn the art of taking as much as is needed for survival and leave the rest to fizzle out.

iii

Stay away from the powerful; they will only use you

The glamour of power is such that many get attracted to it, partly to bask in the glory of others and partly in anticipation of gaining something. But it simply does not work. The mighty and the powerful became so by being individualists and often by stepping on the dreams of others, so they are intrinsically wired to suck others into being where they are.

There is a popular story about a tiger and a small bird where the bird helped the tiger when a bone was stuck in its throat. Some days later, when the hungry bird wanted a small piece of meat from the tiger, he replied, 'Be happy that you came out of my mouth alive. Do not expect anything more.'

Once, I was at one of our centres, which needed some help and support from the Government. I requested a friend to organize a meeting with a powerful politician but he bluntly said, 'Stay away from him. Everyone close to him had to lose. You won't be an exception.'

Yes, the powerful only know how to use the less privileged. If there is a professional relationship, let it be only professional; do not try to make it familiar.

iv

People can be crueller than we can imagine

Expressions like 'back-stabbing' are quite polite compared to how cruel people can be. The famous lines by William Congreve, *'Heaven has no rage like love to hatred turned, Nor hell a fury like a woman scorned,'* may have been used for a particular set of people. But it remains equally applicable to all, even to friends who have no special reason for such cruelty. Why else would Julius Caesar have blurted out *'Et tu, Brutus?'* as his close friend Brutus stabbed him mercilessly to death.

People whom we trust can turn cruel and may make sure that we do not survive or rise ever again. In case we survive, our broodings may ruin our lives. Yes, those whom we trust can harm us beyond our imagination. Once such a betrayal takes place, we need to accept it and then create a new way of life, for they would have made sure that nothing remains intact from our previous way of life.

The trauma and nightmares that may follow are natural fallouts that need to be braved through medication, a support system and inner strength. It is also a good idea to be aware of this. When people are about to behave this way, there is always a perceptible but very subtle change in their behaviour and tone. That is the signal to be alert for the catastrophe.

V

Do not meddle in the Karma of others

Karma, in simple words, means 'acts' or 'results of acts.' Based on the idea of cause and effect, it implies that whatever we do, the results come back to us sooner or later.

In its wider sense Karma means that every act – physical, verbal or mental – leaves an impression which stays with it until the full expression is found at a suitable time and body, implying the idea of rebirth.

The past Karma becomes one of the many forces that decide the result of our present action. Thus, the theory of Karma gives complete freedom of action, where its result will be shaped by our past. One can thus change one's future to a great extent by working constantly on what they do not want in life.

Sometimes our compassion, born out of the plight of being, makes us interfere with the way of others' lives, which often is their Karma. Unless our duty demands that we act, it is better to stay away from meddling, for it may turn out to be harmful for one or both.

In a true incident, once a young lady saw a butterfly struggling to come out of its cocoon. Out of compassion, she broke the shell to help the hexapod. What she did not realize was that the struggle made the butterfly's wings stronger, which, in this case, remained weak. The poor creature could not fly properly and was gobbled up by a bird in no time.

Interfering with Karma is like forcing a stone to fly. The higher it is thrown, the more forcefully it falls. There is no exception to it.

There is an interesting folklore, '*Punah mushiko bhava*,' according to which a sage once saw a mouse running away in fear from a cat. Being powerful, he sprinkled water on it, saying, 'Be a cat' and it turned into a cat. The sage later turned it into various beings to take away its fear and finally made it a tiger, which then pounced upon him. The sage, furious at this, threw water with *'Punah mushiko bhava'* (be a mouse again!).

Indian tradition has innumerable stories to illustrate the idea of not meddling in the Karma of others, since it never works. Just follow your *dharma*, perform your duty and stay away from any kind of personal identification.

As we grow in our power through meditation or materialism, sometimes we become passionate and at other times, we become compassionate, which makes it difficult to handle our own power. That can be dangerous if not directed properly.

But, as mentioned, one has to serve others if it's the line of their duty. And, lending a helping hand is alright but beyond that, it can be dangerous.

vi

Learn to care what others think about you

How often have I heard from the unwise, 'I don't care what others think of me!' While it may sound fair, one should note what others say about us, for they are the best mirrors that we can have to know ourselves. Our mind makes decisions based on external input, so we can neither know nor can we judge ourselves correctly. It is the opinion of others that helps us in setting the course of our lives and act right.

When someone shows respect for what we do, it is then the sign of evolution that we have achieved; while disapproval from those we respect is the sign that things may not be going well.

As for the freelance critics and comment makers, one may ignore them but it is also a good idea to get it verified with our superiors. Otherwise, there is the fear of staying stuck in a rut.

Pause for a moment and think about why someone said something about you!

vii

Sharing secrets

Whom to trust in this world that seems to grow more and more treacherous every day?

One thing that I have learnt in life is that secrets can be shared only with those who too have something to lose if it is out. For example, if we do a seriously wrong thing, then only our family may have something to lose if it comes out to the public. So, a secret is safe only with them. Others may someday turn against us and harm us.

Of course, some saints and sages can keep secrets because they are never going to use it against us.

11

Words

We often fail to realize that words are the most powerful instrument in the world, probably more powerful than the mind when it is taken in the sense of 'idea.' The Greek word for word is 'logos,' which also means 'principles.' In the Bible, it is expressed as: 'In the beginning was the Word and the Word was with God and the Word was God.' (John 1:1).

When the principles of creation become dynamic, the first thing to be created is the cosmic mind, which ultimately appears divided as individual minds. Individual minds can grasp ideas and express them either as they are or as the mind wants to present them. It is important to be judicious with words when we use them and we need to be careful when we listen to them.

i

Words are the verbal persona

The words liberate an idea from the captivity of the mind and have the unlimited potential to sway people. As Shakespeare immortalized the character of Mark Antony in *Julius Caesar* with his famous speech: '*Friends, Romans, countrymen, lend me your* ears.'

We, in India, worship words as Goddess *Vak* or Saraswati, knowing well that our life depends on the words that we choose to express with and how we grasp the intentions of others through their words. After all, words are our verbalized persona; we send and receive powerful data through them.

The way upward is to use words judiciously

and to interpret them correctly. In the *Brihadaranyaka Upanishad,* there is the famous story of '*Da*' where men, gods and the *asuras* go to *Prajapati* (creator God) for guidance. The Lord simply replied, '*Da*' and asked them to reflect on it. The gods felt that it meant '*Damyata,*' self-control; humans understood it as '*Datta,*' charity; and the *asuras* got it as '*Dayadhvam,*' compassion. Through this, God taught them what they lacked.

Later, T.S. Eliot made this expression famous in his poem *The Waste Land.*

Understand a word wrongly and we are doomed. Many disasters take place simply due to this.

ii

Words and acts leak

Life works at three levels: thoughts, words and acts. Words are thus the intermediate stage through which one can understand what a person thinks and what they will do.

Also, when a person wants to do something good or bad, they start talking about it, which is a clear signal of things to come. A person about to indulge in some sinful act always talks about it first, often humorously.

More importantly, words (and acts) have a strange tendency to leak from confidentiality. Written words, being clear acts of commission, are visible to anyone; we often feel that words spoken in confidence to a dear one would remain with them. But no, words leak with time. Sometimes they can cause damage and at other times, they can cause embarrassment.

Since there is a need for expression, words have to be used. The first precaution is to never write anything that, if made public, can cause damage. Second, don't speak such words that, if made public, can cause harm.

One of my teachers often used to say, 'Never talk about the third person. And if you have to, talk only good things about them.'

iii

Don't trust half words

Many years ago, when cars and other motor vehicles were few in number in small towns, I had to arrange for some vehicles for the centre where I was posted. I knew one owner-cum-driver who arranged for other vehicles and said that he would charge just a little extra for an additional trip, which seemed quite normal given that he would have to wait for passengers, make detours and waste time.

Everything went smoothly and all the drivers were paid as per the rate. When it was the turn for the driver whom I knew, he demanded 'that extra' cost of two trips! At the time of fixing the rate, he sounded as if he would charge only for one trip and 'a few rupees extra.' It was embarrassing for me, since I had informed my superiors about the rate, etc.

That day, I vowed not to trust half words in matters of money. Now I never agree to statements like 'you can pay whatever you feel like,' and 'please do what you feel fit.'

And yet, I have fallen into this trap of half-statements repeatedly in other areas, sometimes because of my own expectations and sometimes due to the cleverness of others, which has led me into trouble. The clever ones talk in such a way that you get convinced of something and yet, when the time comes, they claim that they meant something else.

More dangerous is supplying the unspoken half ourselves and concluding that the speaker means one thing when they never meant that. This misunderstanding is often caused when our mind is steeped in an emotion.

A lot of our failings and problems are simply because of our spoken words and half words, but we fail to hear the unspoken ones. Never trust the words that might be half-truths or that may get twisted to mean something different.

iv

Most untrue words imply the desire to be loved

The most clichéd expression in the world, next only to 'I love you,' would probably be 'Don't ever lie to me.' And yet, people lie all the time; those who demand truthfulness and those who are expected to be truthful ... they all lie.

We feel cheated when the lies and fibs by those whom we trust are exposed. But what we fail to appreciate is that people lie to their dear ones only to stay dear to them, for truth has an immensely damaging power.

There indeed are professional cheats and compulsive liars but they are not the subject of this discussion. Here, the explanation is about why we lie and how we should overlook the lies of our dear ones.

Truthfulness is God. A person can realize God through truthfulness. Truth is also a value which we all try to practise and a virtue.

Gandhiji lived by this principle. In Yoga philosophy and in every scripture, truth stands at the top of the ethical values.

However, God is love too. So, whenever there is a conflict between truth and the fear of losing a dear one, people often choose to mask the truth. An understanding mind should be kind to such failings.

There have been occasions when I have been severely reprimanded for not informing my superiors of certain unpleasant happenings and have also been scolded for masking the truth. When asked to explain, I have always felt like blurting out, 'I didn't want to fall in your eyes,' although I always maintained silence, knowing that they may not appreciate what I wanted to say.

When a person does something wrong, they die a thousand deaths. When they try to mask it, they die another thousand deaths. So, keep your relations alive and stay happy with your dear ones with the understanding that half-truths or lies were uttered simply because they love you and they don't want to lose your affection. Period.

V

Unspoken words are silent screams

While it is great to concentrate on one's growth, it is also important to take others along. The importance of community lies in protecting others, too, from falls. One reason for the success of organized religions and systems has been the support for those who seem to lag.

Society has changed a lot due to the advancement of technology. Now, it is not possible to look at someone and know that there is something wrong with them. Instead, we have phones, mails and messages through which we express our joy and fears.

While the spoken words clearly convey the idea, it is the unspoken ones that we should always look for. With no facial presence to gauge the emotions, it is important to catch the silent signals coming through monosyllabic denials.

Once, a friend of mine called me at an odd hour and I missed it. When I called back to ask what the matter was, he said, 'Nothing.' That was a sign that something was seriously wrong. I talked to him about 'weather' and learned the problem, which was pretty serious.

The silence of dear ones is always more eloquent than words. Pay attention to the unspoken.

vi

Save your humour for the close ones

Humour is the sign that we treat someone as our dear one or we consider them inferior to us, which may not always be making fun of them or ridiculing them.

Many banter and use humour with whom they may not be familiar or even in official correspondence. This tendency is dangerous and can cause disaster.

In a very disturbing incident described in the *Ramayana,* there was a demoness Shoorpanakha, who saw Sri Rama while he was living in the forest with his divine consort, Sita and brother, Lakshmana. She approached him with a marriage proposal. Both brothers started exchanging playful words with her, full of innocent humour. Angered at the refusal, she ran towards Sita, saying the problem was her and so she was going to kill her. Shaken, Sri Rama told Lakshmana, 'One should never indulge in fun with the wicked and uncultured.' He then ordered Lakshmana to cut her ears and nose right away.

This incident set the ground for the famous war in Lanka.

Many dreams get crushed under the juggernaut of humour directed towards those who deserve only formality.

vii

A refined language takes us upward

Informality has become the bane of the cyber age, where people have completely forgotten the importance of refined language and choice of words. In earlier times, people with unrefined language were called *anarya* but in the present times, people with refined language are mocked. This speaks volumes about where society is heading.

A refined language becomes subtle and finer, just like music or mathematics in the hands of the maestros. This indicates a state of a high culture and more importantly, a controlled and structured mind.

In the *Ramayana,* we find that when Mahaveer Hanuman first met Sri Rama and Lakshmana, he humbly introduced himself as the minister of Sugreeva, the prince in exile. Sri Rama carefully watched him speak and then commented to Lakshmana about Hanuman:

> One who has not studied *Rig, Yajur* and *Sama veda* cannot pronounce the words with such correctness. Surely he has also studied grammar well, since there has not been a single mistake in his words, although he has spoken a lot. When he was talking, there was not even a little defect found in the eyes, forehead, between his brows or in his other limbs. His expression is not too elaborate, not confusing, not dragging and not very fast. It has risen from his chest and is delivered in a medium tone through his throat. The language he spoke is richly endowed with grammatical purity, is wonderful and auspicious. It is neither too fast nor too slow and it captivates the heart. The three kinds of voice (*urashi* at chest, *shirashi* at head and *kantha* at throat) are wonderful and clear. Whose mind will not be pleased by such a word even if he is an enemy raising a sword?

Impressed, Sri Rama went with Hanuman to meet Sugreeva and the two princes became friends.

Our mind is the only real asset in this world. When controlled, it can make a person attain anything, while an uncontrolled mind is like a car with failed brakes. When a person works on some art for a long time, which includes language, their mind slowly becomes more formatted for higher use.

Failing means an unstructured mind; upward means to regulate it well. This refinement begins well with speech, words and language.

12

Mind and Emotions

Mind, ah! Our only true asset and instrument! Unfortunately, many of us do not pay as much attention to it as we should.

i

Objectivity is a myth

India has dedicated itself to the study of the mind and self for thousands of years. That is how we have Patanjali's *Yoga Sutras* that discuss the mind in detail and the Upanishads that explain the reality of the self and consciousness in entirety. Compared to these, modern science is like a toddler testing its first steps.

According to Indian psychology, the mind works through four stages before it acquires knowledge: data collection, sorting, fixing and finally, identification. These are known as *ahankara* ('I' ness). Thus, when we see something, say in darkness, the mind processes the incoming data through these stages and finally, it decides whether to avoid it or go towards it.

The sense of self-attachment associated with every kind of knowledge makes it impossible for the mind to remain objective towards anything. Although, many Western philosophers, including Aristotle, believe in the infallibility of this kind of knowledge. This is true of science, too, that pretends to be objective in its analysis, while being subjective all the way.

This fundamental folly of considering ourselves to be objective can harm our lives immensely. Likes and dislikes of a person towards something may vary in intensity but they will always be there. So, whenever we feel that we are being 'objective,' particularly during emotional storms, it is imperative to consult someone who is relatively indifferent to that situation.

Making 'objective' decisions during troubled times invariably leads a person into greater trouble, since they then have justification for their acts. The undeniable fact is that only machines can be objective and not a mind.

ii

Beware, the mind creates patterns!

We use digital devices that include video calling. What most of us do not know is that one single picture will take so much space during storage that a phone may not be able to keep it! And yet, any storage device contains a huge number of photographs and videos!

This is made possible by a mathematical tool

known as the Fourier series, which removes unimportant information (like repeated patterns) and also helps in compressing the data.

Our mind works similarly; it creates patterns to avoid being overloaded with data. That is the reason why we skip typing errors while reading something, become prejudiced and judgemental, conclude according to our wishes, etc.

Nassim Nicholas Taleb, a celebrated writer, has explored in his works how we get 'fooled by randomness.' The conflict between randomness and pattern makes a very interesting subject for thinkers and mathematicians.

More importantly, the mind and brain create a dynamic model of the universe, according to the situation. That is how a shooter can hit moving objects and cricket players can take catches while running, etc. A missed target simply means that the dynamic model was not as good as it should have been.

The twin power of the mind, pattern making and dynamic model, can be of great help if put to judicious use. Yet we often fall into their trap, drawing conclusions that suit our whims, projecting our pain or pleasure, living in a make-believe world and clinging to impractical ideology, etc. It is like living in a Quixote world unknowingly.

People with powerful minds and those emotionally charged can suffer from this problem more acutely since they can create patterns and models better than an ordinary mind.

If we ever realize that we have the tendency to conclude or create a lovable heaven for ourselves, then it is a good idea to consult someone outside our circle to set our own course right. Corrections and counterchecks are essential for moving upward.

It is frightening to imagine how many ideologies and religions would collapse if people started using this simple tool!

iii

Divine intervention is a big myth

The great author Somerset Maugham, in his autobiographical novel, *Of Human Bondage,* describes how the protagonist had clubfoot. One night, he prayed to God to set it right. When it did not work the next morning, he stopped believing in God forever!

This episode, although quite touching, reminds us how fragile we are at the mercy of our beliefs that are conditioned and created by the mind! It is not uncommon to hear 'God is in charge,' 'God gave a signal,' 'there was a divine intervention,' etc.

I find all this so amusing, for it all shows how naive we can be and how the mind can trick us into believing simple randomness as a 'divine act' and a 'miracle.' As a kid, it was usual for us to believe in all that, but as grown-ups, it is dangerous to fall into such traps.

Why? That is because God has no favourites

and so He is not troubled by what we are doing and experiencing. The divine intervention, for ordinary people like us, is just a piece that helps us make a better pattern for the mind to observe.

Of course, the great devotees are different. They do not see any human will in anything. For them, everything is the will of God. For the same reason, they do not blame God for their suffering or for the 'ills' of society.

Yes, rationalizing helps us survive. It also puts shackles on us.

iv

Control your mind to control others

Only a handful of thinkers in the West have helped shape the modern mindset of the West. Of these, Marx talked about wealth, Freud about sex and Alfred Adler about the 'alpha male' attitude as the driving force of the individual and society. Probably, none of them had any idea about the Indian spiritual traditions, where even kings and the rich wished to renounce everything and lead their lives dedicated to self-realization.

More importantly, they all failed in realizing that the key to success, whatever the parameter, is the control of one's mind. People wish to command, according to Adler, but to control others, one has to control one's own mind.

Once I had been to India's military academy. Before my visit, I had the silly notion that soldiers are better fighters than officers! So, it was a big shock for me to know that an officer has to be better than those under their charge, in running, shooting, fighting, etc.

This is true of every sphere of our lives. We can have significance and control over others simply by performing better, which requires better mind control. The mind is the only asset that we have. So, its power must not be squandered through emotional indulgence, idle activities, drug abuse and drinking habits.

The charm and power of the greats lie in the

power of their minds and not merely in their pen or sword. Moral and spiritual authority comes only through complete control over one's mind.

V

Emotions

Emotions are the glue that binds us to an idea. Thus, they are neither good nor bad and neither positive nor negative. At best, they propel an idea to move forward with power. So, one has to be careful of their emotions and also of the emotions of others.

We all have good and bad aspects in our personality. When we move with people, they usually do not speak ill of us. This often makes us conclude that others have a good opinion about us, which may not be true. So, the arousal of emotions can cause havoc.

There is a very poignant incident in the *Mahabharata* that illustrates the devastating power of words aroused out of poking at emotions. During the Kurukshetra war, Yudhisthira had to run away from the battlefield because of his defeat at the hands of Karna. Hearing this, Arjuna left the battlefield and came to see if his elder brother was safe. Yudhisthira mistakenly thought that Karna had been neutralized but it was not so. Frustrated, he used harsh words towards Arjuna, which made him draw his sword to kill Yudhisthira, saying that he had sworn that he would kill anyone who insults his capabilities!

The resolutions that we make!

Sri Krishna then intervened and asked Arjuna to insult his elder brother, which would be like death for him and then fall at his feet to apologize for the transgression. Willy-nilly, Arjuna spoke his mind out, calling Yudhisthira a 'coward,' 'gambler' and 'braggart who talked big sitting on the bed of his wife!'

Having said what he had to, Arjuna fell at Yudhisthira's feet, crying torrentially and seeking an apology.

Every word that Arjuna had spoken was true but he had lost the armour of respect because of misplaced emotions. A devastated Yudhisthira then wanted to commit suicide but was somehow persuaded by the Lord not to do so.

One big lesson that I have learnt in my life, after a thousand stumbles and stabs, has been not to arouse the emotions of anger in others and to go quiet, completely quiet, when angry, for the outcome of bared words would be unpredictable.

vi

Flowers in the sky

We usually gain knowledge through our senses and logical inferences. On the other hand, we land in the mire of false understanding mainly through imagination. In worst cases, one may conclude the impossible, like there are flowers in the sky, too.

One funny incident that happened to me was when I was a young student. Once, I was reading a storybook during study hours when a very intelligent and strict teacher caught me. He seized the book and took it with him. I was so scared of the consequences that I avoided him as much as I could. When it was time to return the book to the library, I told the librarian that I had lost the book! He refused to believe it and asked me to search for it everywhere. The holidays had come, so it had to be done right away.

With terror written all over me, I went to meet the teacher and asked sheepishly for the book. He said, 'Oh, I was waiting for you to come and collect it.' You can imagine my relief and gratitude towards him.

Our mind imagines something and then reinforces it with the concrete emotions such as fear, shame, hatred, desire, anger, greed, expectations, arrogance and jealousy. Once emotion enters the arena, the little objective understanding that we may have becomes more and more opaque. So, it is always better to go forward and face it or take the help of someone close to us.

13

Success

i

The internal and external of success

Everyone wants success but a rare few know its anatomy and physiology, i.e., what success is and how it is attained.

The true measure of success for anyone is when the person striving for it loses the measure of it. So, for an author, true success would be if they cannot say for sure how many works they have created!

Under normal conditions, a person sets their goal on having some wealth, house, etc. But that is ordinary compared to when a person loses count. In Indian lore, it is said that Kubera, the demigod who lords over wealth, has no idea of how much wealth he has. This level of success can be achieved if someone works towards what they like or want. The unstoppable juggernaut of their effort would then bring the uncountable success.

The second test is when one's success makes their name a verb instead of being merely a noun. In the early twentieth century, there was a saying in the USA, 'as rich as Rockefeller,' which has now become an idiom. Similarly, patience and non-violence in India are often termed as '*Gandhigiri,*' implying the principles of Gandhiji.

If one has the desire to be successful, it better be on these lines, for the long haul. The Yoga philosophy puts this idea beautifully in one of its aphorisms, 'Success (in Yoga) is attained through a persistent effort for a long time.'

As a young person, I too believed in immediate results and quick success but now

I know better. Those who we consider to be prodigies or a success story must have practised their skill from birth, which cannot be matched by the ordinary. So, to dream of quick success is a guarantee of failure and pain.

ii

Planned things do not make a splash

The mushrooming of management institutions, catering to the insane desire for success, has instilled in the minds of the young the conviction that they will succeed. This desire gets further fanned when the success stories of others are splashed over the media.

I have met quite a few young aspiring authors calculating the royalty that they would get and the fame that would walk ahead of them, even before they have written a book! They do have an idea or two for the book but that is enough to take them into the world of fantasies, with no palpable result.

While success or achievement, leading to bread and butter, may be made possible through planning and effort, true success always comes without any plan. When a person remains steadfast to an ideal, devoting themselves to it for years, a splash would be visible over time and distance. But the inkling of it can never be made beforehand.

It indeed is a strange law of nature that it takes away the power from an act when it is well planned.

So, how to succeed? The Indian way of life says, gather your spread, focus on your ideal, dedicate yourself for an undefined length of time and most importantly, forget the outcome forever.

iii

Popularity is not everything

In a very interesting study offered by *Time* magazine, it ranked famous people in the order of popularity in its 1950 edition and declared Winston Churchill as the man of the half-century. When the same magazine brought out the list of the top ten persons of the century, his name was nowhere in the list, while Gandhi Ji's name was at the second spot, after that of Einstein. It was the same Gandhi Ji whom Churchill had called a half-naked fakir and had put him in jail many times.

So, can popularity ever be the test of success? No.

There is a popular story in which a creeper reached the top of a bamboo plant and asked, 'How long did it take you to reach here?' 'Sixty years,' said the tree. 'Oh, that long! See how I have reached here in three months.' After a month, the creeper was nowhere to be seen.

The present frenzy to succeed through social media is actually taking people downward, whereas the true goal should be to move upward through one's failings. Immature minds do not realize that they are behaving like the creeper in the above-mentioned story and they won't know what has hit them once their popularity wanes.

The real success resonates in every home, even after a long time. When the great sage Valmiki was writing *Ramayana,* could he have ever imagined that his work would be translated into so many languages and adapted for various kinds of performances? It is doubtful.

Of course, not every author can be Valmiki but the goal is to move on from popularity to dedication to something higher than 'food, fight, flight, procreation.'

iv

People should shed tears when we are down

There is a saying that the number of people attending someone's funeral shows the kind of life they had lived. While alive, one may have their failings, criticisms, attacks, etc. but at heart, people know what kind of person someone has been.

This is true for life, too. People should shed tears when we fail or fall due to our mistakes or for no fault of ours. In a very touching incident, described in the *Ramayana*, when Sri Rama was sent to exile for fourteen years for no fault of his. The people of Ayodhya, his capital city, walked behind him vowing never to return without him.

This incident is more than inspirational. Our acts and behaviour should be such that people around us, unless threatened by the evil forces, would shed tears and offer to walk with us, instead of muttering, 'serves him right.' This is one good sign of a life lived well.

V

Success is running after us

Since our childhood, we are trained to believe in the 'Cause and Effect' theory, according to which success comes to those who 'aspire and struggle.' Some people also add 'talent' to the prerequisite list. The ever-increasing materialistic outlook is enforcing these crude ideas on life more and more.

The fact is that we are one with the highest powers of the world and so we can attain anything, control anything; we only need to develop the power to hold it when it comes. Indeed, success is running after us, screaming to find a worthy candidate but we fail it.

An interesting story from the ancient traditions illustrates it well.

Once, the gods and the *asuras* agreed to churn the ocean and get *amrita* from it. Huge arrangements were made for that, in which all the mighty and powerful joined. Lord Vishnu took the form of the *Kurma avatar*, a tortoise, to hold the churner, a mountain, on his back. Being the Lord, he was also present there as an onlooker along with the divine sages.

The churning produced many things one after another. At one point, Lakshmi, the goddess of wealth, splendour and success, came out. She looked around to find the right one for her but she was not happy with anyone. And then she saw Lord Vishnu, calm but powerful, appealing but detached, active but desireless. She chose the Lord and became his divine consort.

The terms for splendour and Lakshmi are the same: *Sri*. Thus, *Sri,* in the form of wealth, fame and success, wants to garland us but, seeing us unworthy, moves away from us.

All aspirations and struggles are meant to make us fit to hold *Sri*. Or else, like a weak wire getting burnt by high voltage, we too would be burnt if *Sri* came to us. There are so many examples around us of when an unworthy person got power or wealth but it ruined them.

Do not aspire for success; only strive to acquire competence.

14

Unlimiting Oneself

Life is often seen as a journey. But what kind of journey is life? Is it like earth-bound travels or is it like going beyond the bond of gravity?

Any journey, undertaken by whatever mode, requires more or less the same kind of preparation. Thus, whether the travel is by train, bus, car or flight, the things that we need to carry are more or less the same. More importantly, the guidance required for the first time travel or the mode of transport is minimal.

However, imagine that we are lucky enough to be selected for a space voyage, breaking the bonds of gravity. The training that would then be required would be qualitatively different and the commodities to be carried would have no similarity with what we are used to carrying. In the journey of life, too, the preparations would vary according to how we treat life.

Seen closely, the Indian way of life views life journey not as earth-bound but as a venture beyond gravity, with a different attitude and preparation aimed at breaking free from the comfort zone and in some exceptional cases, the goal is beyond the empires of the mind!

In simple terms, it means to be spiritual, and to unlimit oneself.

i

Ideals as aid to growth

A big part of my life has been spent handling students at various educational institutions, so I have a fair share of understanding of how the young minds work.

In earlier times, young students often named some great personalities as their ideals, which probably used to be mere parroting. Now, the fig leaf of ideals is gone. They often say that either parent is their ideal. A truly funny phenomenon these days is to hear statements like 'my father is the best father in the world!' These naive people cannot even distinguish between their liking and their ideal!

People expect to grow and succeed even when they have no ideal!

The idea of an ideal can be best understood by the example of crystal making. When the crystal of some substance is to be made, impure crystals are put in the solvent until it becomes saturated. The solution is then heated to increase its capacity and then more crystals are added to the solvent. When crystals cannot be added anymore, it is then known as a supersaturated solution. After that, a pure crystal is added to it. Lo and behold! New crystals start forming around the pure crystal. Interestingly, their purity is the same as the crystal that was put externally in the supersaturated solution.

Ideals are exactly like crystallization: we acquire knowledge as we grow, which is like pouring impure crystals; then we work hard in life, which is like heating the solvent; after that, we gain more knowledge and work more; and finally, we latch on to an ideal to make a pure crystal of ourselves.

To be great, one has to have a perfect ideal, knowledge and hard work. Lack of any of these would mean that we would end up with an impure and imperfect life.

ii

Staying power comes through ideal

One important reason for failing in life is that we don't have the staying power; we just go with the flow without knowing what we are doing and why.

There is a funny story about Lord Shiva and a farmer who had nothing else other than a small piece of land. Once, for some reason, Shiva became angry with that part of the country and said that there would be no rain until he blew his conch. After a few years, the Lord came to see how things were. He was surprised to see that one farmer was tilling his land. So, he approached the farmer in the garb of another farmer and commented, 'There is going to be no rain in this part, so why are you tilling it?'

'I may forget my skill,' said the farmer.

This worried the Lord, thinking that if he did not blow his conch for a long time, he might then forget how to blow it! He immediately blew the conch and there was the rain.

No story can ever prove a point but they serve as very good pointers. It is the same with this story. The farmer had only one skill and he had only one ideal. He stuck to it even amidst the worst of famine.

Yes, power comes only when a person has an impersonal ideal and success comes to those who grow well on those lines.

iii

Person, personality, principles

One of the stories from Lord Buddha's life touched me deeply. Once, his favourite disciple, Ananda, was out begging when he felt thirsty and asked a lady for water from the well. She told him that she was of low caste, to which Ananda said that he had asked for water and not her caste.

Mesmerized by his kind words, the lady whose name was Prakriti, walked behind him to be with him forever. When Lord Buddha learned of this incident, he called her and asked what she liked about him. 'Compassion,' said she. Practise it yourself and you too will become great, said the Lord.

The parable goes on to say how Prakriti became a great nun after practising the ideal.

Love comes in three forms: person, personality and principles. When we set an ideal, which means to have a mould for ourselves, we often fix our eyes on people and personalities and not on the principles.

Disillusionment, despair, failing and falling come simply because we get glued to a person or a personality. Anyone who loves a principle and has that for an ideal can never fail. There can be setbacks but never a failure for them.

Who is a person? Or a personality? Both are physical representations and a bad one, of a principle. Even in religion, a person has to move from loving, say, Lord Krishna, the personality, to Lord Krishna, the principle. His personality has been portrayed in many sacred books which are narrated and sung. People find those stories fascinating but forget that the principles that he represents are more important, universal and above all, good or bad.

When we love someone, we rarely love their personality and soon degrade ourselves by loving the person. In some rare cases, we first love a person and then move on to love their personality. Lucky are those who love the principles. A beautiful face is of a person who may have a wonderful personality. Its impersonal aspect lies in 'beauty,' which is God.

To unlimit ourselves, we need to focus more on principles than anything else.

iv

Impersonal pursuits

Dialogues by Plato is famous for his philosophical outpourings but the more striking content are the words of Socrates. One of the great ideas given by the philosopher is of 'Beauty,' where he relates it to goodness.

When read closely, Socrates was talking about the impersonal aspect of an idea. His theory of Forms is about ideals existing independently of physical forms or expressions. The goal is to focus on the impersonal instead of the personal, bound by the constraints of time, space and matter.

In India, the sages gave us a clear idea about the impersonal and the personal. When God wants to create, He appears as God in a form and then His three essential aspects, existence, knowledge and joy, intermix to create abstract ideas which, when verbalized, become spoken words and when they get a form, they are known as bodies.

The world is the play of name and form, words and bodies. Behind it lies the eternal, impersonal idea of existence, knowledge and bliss. The goal of life is to move from the personal aspects of name and form to the impersonal truths.

For example, we all loved toys and games when we were kids. As we grew up, our objects of love kept changing but the act of love remained the same. So, to grow upward, one needs to focus on love, instead of the object of love. Similarly, one needs to focus on pure knowledge i.e., God, instead of the books we derive knowledge from.

The best way to move upward is to realize

one's area of strength, think of the impersonal truth behind it and then centre one's activities around it. There can be no person in the world who does not have some area of strength and hence everyone can become great.

Due to the same reason, every act, word or thought is an expression of the divine and so any pursuit at its highest level becomes divine; it becomes unlimited. That is the reason why Indian tradition treats singing, dancing, any other art and every act as a connection to God. Nothing is prohibited in India; nothing is worldly.

V

Limited, unlimited

René Descartes was a French philosopher who gave us the idea of a graph with an X-axis and a Y-axis. Philosophically, it is known as the Cartesian divide, where God and world, mind and matter, etc., have a divide and so sacred and secular (i.e. worldly) are completely separate.

India sees existence as a whole and hence there is no scope for the Cartesian divide here: sacred-secular conflict, Nationalism-Dharma dilemma, etc. Whatever is, it simply is. The desire and act that is limited or confined, makes one worldly, while the unlimited aspect of everything and every act is God.

Unfortunately, the people of India have forgotten this ideal. What to say then of preaching it to the world! One main reason for the downfall of India and suffering in the world is that we do not practise this truth of no Cartesian divide; God alone exists and infinity alone exists.

India says, 'Arise! You have all the knowledge and all the strength within you, so give up the idea that you are limited or chained. Throw away all your weaknesses and be free! The world is the place where we gain good and bad experiences, only to move upward and forward towards our true nature, which is eternal, infinite and joyful. Be brave, be bold. Move on!'

Om Shantih!